OXFORD ENGLISH

QUEST

Q
★
Y6/P7

COMPANION 4

ELAINE CANHAM

Contents

UNIT 1

Superhero saves the world!

EXTREMITY MAN — 4

Meet ... Extremity Man 4
Deep sea dilemma: Mariana Trench 6
Life in the freezer: Verkhoyansk 10
Drama in Death Valley 12
Dripping in Cherrapunji 14
Sizzling Atacama Desert 15
Ending on Everest 16

UNIT 2

Double, double, toil and trouble; fire burn, and cauldron bubble ...

Something Wicked This Way Comes *by Lesley Densham* — 18

Introduction 18
William Shakespeare 1564–1616 18
Macbeth medley 20
Macbeth: Act 4, Scene 1 *by William Shakespeare* 24
Samuel Pepys 1633–1703 26
The Great Plague 1665–1671 28
The Great Fire of London 1666 31

UNIT 3

What have you got in common with a pencil, a barbecue and a diamond ring?

Carbon Copy — 34

Introduction 34
Carbon casebook 34
Charcoal – then and now 36
Are we burning dead dinosaurs? 38
The origins of oil 40
The dangers of carbon 42
Sparkly, spooky diamonds 44
The Jeweller's Clever Daughter *by Adèle Geras* 46
Carbon-planet poems 48

UNIT 4

Are you sitting comfortably?

Sensational Shorts — 50

A Whole New Life *by Sally Prue* 50
The Chase *by Hazel Marshall* 52
The Mayan Man of Gold *retold by Chris Buckton* 54
Isaiah, Chapter 46 55
The Great Cake Disaster *by Chris Buckton* 56
The Fallen Angel Cake *by Maggie Pearson* 57
In the Back Seat *by Kevin Crossley-Holland* 58
Room for One More *by Kevin Crossley-Holland* 59
Buddha and the Swan *retold by Robert Fisher* 60
Who? *by Chris Buckton* 62
The Last Thylacine *by Jan Andrew Henderson* 64

UNIT 5

It's right to be right about rights. Right?

Rights — 66

Introduction 66
Should you be able to vote at 16? 66
Why do we have to wear a uniform? 68
What's so good about going to school? 70
We know our rights – so what? 72
Is advertising bad for us? 74
What can we do about bullying? 76
Rights *by Helena Pielichaty* 78

UNIT 6

Did you know that when you sneeze, bits wheeze out of your nose as fast as an intercity express train?

Celebrate Your Senses — 80

Coming to our senses 80
The eyes have it 82
Let's hear it for our ears 84
Rising to the challenge 86
A feeling for art 88
Strange smells of success 90
In touch with our skin 92

INDEX 94

Extremity Man
Meet ... Extremity Man

From the Government's Top Secret files:

Name: Xavier Xenon
Code name: Extremity Man
Occupation: Superhero
Mission: To go to extremes (and save the world)

Extremity Man is as:

* cool as a polar bear in sunglasses;
* hot as a chilli pepper in a volcano;
* fast as a cheetah on a laser jet;
* strong as a herd of bionic elephants;
* brave as a gladiator fighting a force field;
* stealthy as a snowflake in the desert;
* clever as a brain plugged into the universe;
* cunning as a scorpion in a sandcastle.

He's extraordinary!
He's exciting!
He's exactly what you need
when you're in trouble!

Extremity Man will visit the most extreme places in the world, including:
- ☀ the sheerest rock face;
- ☀ the most treacherous whirlpool;
- ☀ the deepest deep-sea crater;
- ☀ the most sizzling desert;
- ☀ the coldest ice floe;
- ☀ the most poisonous cave.

Quotes from satisfied customers

I was 5000m down, with the last bubble of air in my tank, and my flipper stuck in a fangtooth's mouth, when I made the call. Within a nanosecond, Extremity Man was there! **D.S. Diver**

Inside the volcano's throat is a lava lake and magma chamber - full of boiling liquid that feeds the volcano. As I took temperature readings, the volcano started to swallow - and I would have been gulped, then fired sky-high when it erupted. Just as my thermometer melted, Extremity Man steamed along. Cool! **V. Esuvius**

I was at the centre of the Earth, about to go back up, when a curtain of fire closed me off. It would have been curtains for me if it hadn't been for Extremity Man. (Remember kids, never play with fire). **Name withheld**

One small step, one giant leap – and I was about to fall off the Highlands of the moon. Before I had time to radio Houston, Extremity Man came into orbit. Meteoric. **N. Armstrong**

crater

lava flow

throat

side vent

layers of lava and ash

rock layers of the Earth's Crust

magma chamber

Deep Sea Dilemma: Mariana Trench

Location: *High in the Austrian Alps, an old schloss sits on a mountain top. Inside, Xavier Xenon, the mysterious owner, is sitting in his library studying an ancient manuscript.*

Butler: Call for you, sir.

Telephone: Xavier? This is X. We have an extreme situation. Someone is trying to plant a bomb in the Mariana Trench.

Xavier: The deepest place in the world? That could start the biggest earthquake in history. Have no fear, X, I'm on my way.

Thinks: *The Mariana Trench, hmm. Now what do I know about that …*

> I NEED TO CONSULT MY XTREME FACT FILE. A SUPERHERO IS ONLY AS GOOD AS HIS FACTS.

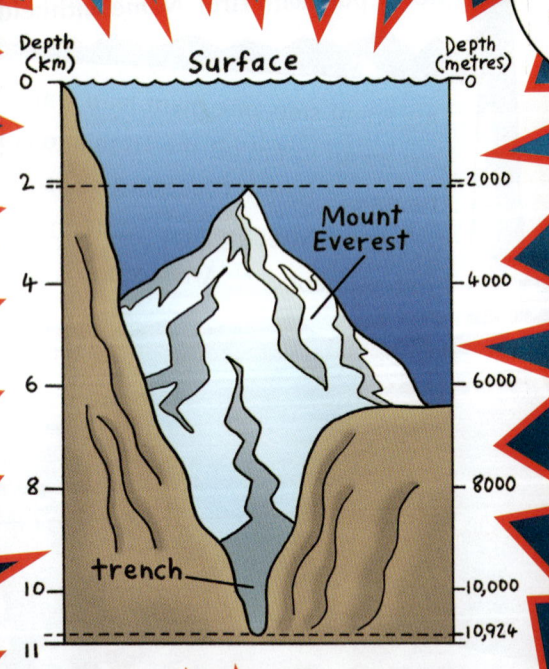

Xtreme Fact File: The Mariana Trench contains the deepest place in the world – the Challenger Deep. It is 10,924 m or almost 11 km deep. If you could drop Mount Everest into it, there would still be about 2 km of sea water over the top of the mountain.

The Mariana Trench is near the Philippines. It is in the biggest ocean on Earth, the Pacific, which stretches all the way from the Antarctic to the Arctic. On the floor of the trench, the water pressure is more than 1 ton per square centimetre.

The deepest part of the Mariana Trench, the Challenger Deep, got its name because it was found in 1951 by the Royal Navy ship *Challenger*.

In 1960, the US Navy sent the *Trieste*, a mini-submarine designed to go really deep, down into the Mariana Trench to see just how far it would go. There were two men inside, US Navy officer Lt Don Walsh and Swiss scientist Jacques Piccard. After five hours, they touched bottom at 10,915 m, the deepest anyone has ever been. They returned safely to the surface and, more than 40 years later, no one else has equalled their record.

While on the bottom, Jacques Piccard swore he saw a fish swimming past the window, but he doesn't know what it was.

US Navy officer Lt Don Walsh and Swiss scientist Jacques Piccard took more than five hours in the Trieste *mini-submarine (above) to get to the bottom of the Mariana Trench.*

SURVIVAL IN THE DEEP

Sunlight can't reach deeper than about 200 m below the surface of the sea, but there are many kinds of fish that have specially adapted to living under such pressure and in such darkness. Many can make their own light, either by growing luminescent bacteria in special body pockets, or by producing light in their own body organs – these personal 'light bulbs' are called photophores. Many fish down here survive on scraps that sink down from above – or sometimes they eat each other.

Freaky Fish

Most viper fish (found at depths of up to 1600 m – about a mile down), are completely black, except for their photophores ('light bulbs'), which they use to lure fish they want to attack and eat.

Some fish are completely see-through, so that they blend in with the dim light to avoid being caught by predators. They also have really big eyes, to gather as much light as possible.

Other fish in the depths include the gulper eel, which has a hinged skull, huge mouth, and a stretchy stomach so that it can attack and eat fish as big as itself. The giant grenadier fish lives about 7000 m down. It is a very smelly fish and swims slowly over the seabed searching for live prey, as well as dead things to eat. The fangtooth (also known as the ogrefish) has teeth so big that it can't close its mouth.

Earthquake averted – Extremity Man dives down deep

Extremity Man's exit for Mr Evil

I'LL DETONATE IT WHEN IT'S A FEW MILES DOWN ...

... THE SHOCKWAVES WILL GO RIGHT THROUGH THE EARTH'S CRUST. NO ONE CAN STOP ME NOW!

WANT TO BET, MR.EVIL?

YOU'RE TOO LATE, EXTREMITY MAN. EVEN YOU CAN'T SAVE THE WORLD NOW. HA HA!

gulper eel

giant grenadier fish

Living at around 2 km deep, this fish is almost all mouth. The gulper eel can unhinge its enormous jaws and stretch its stomach to eat a fish as big as itself.

Fish belonging to the brotulid family are thought to be the world's deepest-living fish. One (*Abyssobrotula galatheae*) was found in the Caribbean Sea in the Puerto Rican Trench at a depth of 8372 m (that's over five miles down). They don't seem to have any eyes (what's the point, if you live in the dark?) and they probably have other highly developed senses – but scientists know next to nothing about them.

Mayhem in the Mariana – but Extremity Man saves the day!

**Extremity Man 1
Mr Evil 0**

Superhero trounces trench trasher

YOU'RE EXTRAORDINARILY GOOD AT THIS, BUT YOU SHOULDN'T PUSH YOURSELF TO SUCH EXTREMES!

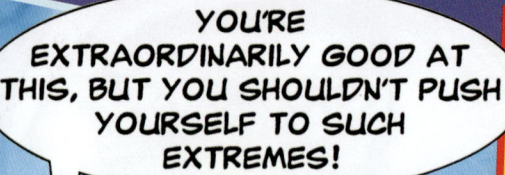

Some time later ... Extremity Man is doing his exercises.

Gym instructor: That was excellent. You're extraordinarily good at this, Mr Xenon. But you shouldn't push yourself to such extremes.

Extremity Man: I'm an extreme kind of guy.

His mobile goes off.

X: Xavier? This is X. Mr Evil has escaped. We have him cornered, but we need your help.

Extremity Man: Name the place and I'll be there.

X: He's near Verkhoyansk, the coldest town on the planet. And his car has broken down. He won't last long in that extreme cold, but he thinks his sidekicks are on the way to rescue him.

Extremity Man: I'm always in favour of dropping in on an old acquaintance. I'm on my way.

ARCTIC CIRCLE

Yana River

Verkhoyansk

SIBERIA

I NEED TO CONSULT MY XTREME FACT FILE. A SUPERHERO IS ONLY AS GOOD AS HIS FACTS.

Xtreme Fact File: Verkhoyansk is the coldest place where people live in the world. It is in Siberia (Russia), on the Yana River, near the Arctic Circle. In 1996, scientists there recorded the lowest ever natural temperature of –68° C.

Many people in and around Verkhoyansk work in the fur trade, or breed reindeer.

Russian rulers used to send people they didn't like to Verkhoyansk and make them build roads.

When the cold weather starts, people who live in Verkhoyansk hang raw fish and raw horsemeat in bags outside their houses. When they want to eat, they just bring it in, slice it and eat it with black pepper and vodka. The extreme cold kills any bacteria just as well as cooking would.

The river in Verkhoyansk is frozen solid for most of the year. A heavily insulated pipeline is kept up in the air, to provide hot and cold water and sanitation.

The sun sets at about 2 p.m. in winter. It is so cold that lots of people walk backwards, to reduce the effect of the wind on their faces. If you see patches of white appearing on someone's skin, it's the beginning of frostbite. Even a few minutes in the cold can lead to frostbite on exposed skin. If you spit outside in winter in Verkhoyansk, your saliva will be frozen solid before it lands.

Primary school children don't go to school if the temperature is below −48° C, while secondary school pupils stay off if the temperature reaches −50° C. It's the law!

Cars can only be used in winter if they are kept in heated garages. Drivers who park their cars outside have to leave them running. Cars have double glazing and special blankets for their engines.

On a frozen river near Verkhoyansk, Mr Evil is questioning the wisdom of his sidekick.

IF I COULD GET THIS BLOWTORCH TO WORK, I COULD WARM UP THE ENGINE.

YOU IDIOT! NUMBSKULL!

IF WE DON'T GET RESCUED SOON, WE'RE GOING TO DIE OF COLD!

HAVE NO FEAR, MR EVIL, HELP IS HERE!

NOT SO FAST MR E. DON'T YOU KNOW, EXTREME TEMPERATURES HAVE NO EFFECT ON ME?

WHERE ... UH ... WHERE ARE WE GOING?

NO! NOT EXTREMITY MAN!

GIVE ME THAT BLOWTORCH!

NOW IT'S A 'BOW' TORCH.

TO THE HOTTEST PLACE ON EARTH!

Drama in Death Valley

Xtreme Fact File: Death Valley in California, USA, is thought to be the hottest place on Earth, with scientists recording a temperature there of 57° C. The Libyan desert in Africa is said to have reached 58° C in 1936, but scientists argue over whether this was recorded properly.

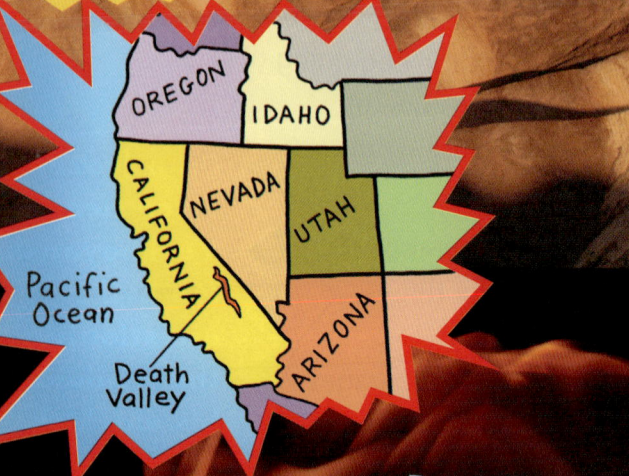

OREGON

IDAHO

CALIFORNIA

NEVADA

UTAH

Pacific Ocean

Death Valley

ARIZONA

The biggest town in the area, Rhyolite, which is just outside the Death Valley park boundary, was built in 1904. At one time, it had a population of 10,000. It had hotels, shops, a stock exchange, a hospital and a big factory to refine the ore from the gold mine. But by 1911 the mine had closed, and in 1916, the last person left.

There is lots of wildlife in the valley, including rattlesnakes, scorpions, mountain lions, bobcats, badgers and even descendants of the mules the prospectors brought with them all those years ago.

The average temperature in July is 46°C, and although there is little average rainfall, there is always the risk of flash floods.

Death Valley is a national park and contains more than 8000 km² of wilderness.

It was called Death Valley after people joining the gold rush in 1849 decided to travel through the area to get to the gold fields in western California. They got lost, endured months of hardship, had to slaughter the oxen that drew their wagons for food, and were saved from dying of thirst only by a snowstorm – but they made it.

There are several ghost towns in the valley, where people once lived and mined for gold, silver, copper and lead.

Extremity Man goes Missing!

Superhero with Mr Evil as blast rocks Death Valley

FEARS were growing last night for the fate of Extremity Man, thought to have been killed in a gigantic blast with Mr Evil.

The mysterious superhero, who arrested Mr Evil in Siberia, was last seen with his unspeakable adversary in Death Valley, California, the hottest place on Earth.

A spokesman for Britain's Prime Minister said yesterday, "We fear the worst, but hope for the best. If anyone could survive that blast in a place like Death Valley, it would be Extremity Man, but who knows what fiendish invention Mr Evil has up his sleeve?"

The last sighting of Extremity Man was early yesterday morning, as he flew over the Death Valley park reception centre, clutching Mr Evil and a sidekick. A few minutes later there was a tremendous explosion, and rescue teams who were sent out have found evidence of intense heat. No one knows what caused the explosion.

"It's a complete mystery," said one park ranger. "But there would be nothing left of anyone caught in that blast. I don't know if even Extremity Man could have stood that heat."

Story in depth: pages 2, 3, 4, 5, 6, 7, 8, 9, 10, 11, 12, 15.

Dripping in Cherrapunji

Deadly bomb

To... | Mr X
Cc... |
Subject: | Deadly bomb

Hi X,

Well, here I am in Cherrapunji, India, the wettest place on the planet and I must say it's a nice change from extreme heat; very soothing, in fact.

That fiendish Mr Evil had a new deadly type of bomb in his backpack, and he detonated it just as we were flying over Death Valley. I don't know what happened to Mr Evil, or his sidekick. I can't believe he's dead, but the blast was so extreme, even for me, that I was knocked out into the ionosphere. But I am a superhero after all, and I should be able to go to any extreme.

When I am back to full health, I shall go looking for Mr Evil. I won't rest until I know the full truth of what happened.

Cherrapunji, the wettest place on Earth

Travellers to India would be mad to miss out on this marvellous experience. Cherrapunji is 1400m up in the heart of the northern state of Meghalaya – the abode of clouds. It never stops raining here, from the gentle patter of raindrops in the winter, to the full-blown monsoons of May to September. There is no month without rain, but locals insist that it rains mostly at night. The average annual rainfall is 10,871mm. Botanists will delight in the rare orchids, ferns and moss which grow freely everywhere. There are several comfortable private hotels. Call us now to arrange a trip … You'd be wet not to go!

Sizzling Atacama Desert

Mr Evil

To... Mr X

CC...

Subject: Mr Evil

Hi X,

Thought I'd check out the driest place on Earth. Even I felt a bit soggy in Cherrapunji, but am definitely on the mend. Have there been any sightings of Mr Evil?

Xavier

Xtreme Fact File: The Atacama Desert is on the coast of Chile, South America - right next to the Pacific Ocean. Much of it is in the Andes mountains, and is very high. It can be quite cold, too, with average daily temperatures between 0°C and 25°C. In some parts of the desert it hasn't rained for 400 years. There are some salt lakes, and small patches of snow right in the highest peaks, but most moisture is provided by fogs that roll in from the Pacific.

NORTH AMERICA

Atlantic Ocean

Pacific Ocean

Andes Mountains

SOUTH AMERICA

Atacama Desert (CHILE)

SOME DAYS LATER ...

XAVIER? WE WANT YOU TO GO TO A TIBETAN MONASTERY ON THE SLOPES OF EVEREST. IT SEEMS THE MONKS THERE MIGHT HAVE A CURE FOR THE EFFECT THAT BOMB HAD ON YOU.

YOU MEAN I COULD GO TO EXTREMES AGAIN ... AND BEYOND? I'M ON MY WAY, X.

Something Wicked This Way Comes

by Lesley Densham

Introduction

Ever thought you had bad luck? Spare a thought for many of Shakespeare's characters who often had horrible things happen to them. Or, worse still, for Londoners in the 17th century. In just 12 months they had plague, war and a great fire. How unlucky is that?!

William Shakespeare 1564–1616

William Shakespeare was an English playwright and poet who lived from 1564 to 1616. His plays are performed in hundreds of languages all over the world, and he is known as one of the greatest writers of all time. In the 40 or so plays that he wrote, Shakespeare wrote about human nature, and how people behave. That is why, although his words can be hard to understand, his plays are as popular today as they were 400 years ago.

Stone monument to William Shakespeare in the Holy Trinity Church, Stratford-upon-Avon

Shakespeare's birthplace in Henley Street, Stratford-upon-Avon

DARLING WIFE   STOP   MET WITCHES ON HEATH STOP
I'M TO BE KING OF SCOTLAND STOP
WHAT'LL HAPPEN TO DUNCAN I WONDER   STOP   BACK SOON
STOP   MACBETH XXX

Dear diary,

Macbeth is to be king! Then I shall be Queen of Scotland! But I don't want to wait. King Duncan may be old, but who knows how much longer he can last? And what's more, if he stays on the throne for much longer, his son Malcolm will be old enough to be king after him. No, we must act! Macbeth may be a hero in battle, but he won't want to kill Duncan. I can't possibly do it myself, because Duncan looks too much like my father, so Macbeth will have to do it! I'll make him screw up his courage.

Macbeth must kill Duncan. I will drug the guards, then, when Macbeth has finished with the king, he can kill the guards and claim that they were the murderers! The perfect crime!

SCOTTISH DAILY NEWS
MURDER MOST FOUL
King Duncan is dead
by our royal correspondent

As noble King Duncan lay asleep last night in the castle of his friend, Macbeth, he was fatally stabbed. The loyal and grieving Macbeth stated, "It was dreadful. I was woken from a deep sleep by a cry of 'Murder!' I recognised my long-time friend, Duncan's, voice. So I ran. I was just in time to see the two scheming men who should have been guarding him sneaking out of his chamber with a bloodstained dagger. Of course, I had to kill them. Then I went in to see my esteemed King, Duncan. And he was dead. I am distraught!"

After the death of his father, young Prince Malcolm decided that his own life was in danger, so he has fled for England leaving his father's brave and heroic friend, Macbeth, to be crowned King of Scotland.

LONG LIVE KING MACBETH!

Have you heard about all the unnatural things that are happening at the moment? First, there are these storms. Then, it is said that a hunting falcon was killed by a mere owl, and that Duncan's beautiful horses went mad and started eating each other, even as the old King was murdered.

Hail Macduff

Witches' Weekly

Macbeth cannot be beaten – hot off the press!

by our Blasted Heath correspondent

King Macbeth met again with the bewitching trio of sisters on the heath last night. They gave him the good news. Once the glorious girls had gone, Macbeth gave an exclusive interview.

"Well, they said that I just can't be beaten. Of course, being witches, they didn't say it quite in those words, but what they did say was that I can't be beaten unless 'Great Birnam Wood to high Dunsinane Hill shall come' (and let's face it, when is a forest ever going to march towards a hill – especially Dunsinane Hill which has my castle on its top?). They also said that, 'None of woman born shall harm Macbeth', and since every man is born of a woman then no one can beat me! Simple really.

The only bit that worries me is that they said that I should beware Macduff. He's a general in my army, but I'm not sure how loyal to me he is. He was very close to Duncan. I may just have to kill his wife and children to keep him in line! … But don't put that in your paper!"

Later, I caught up with the winsome women and talked to them. According to Witch 1, "It was even better than last time. We did all that 'Double, double, toil and trouble; Fire burn, and cauldron bubble' stuff – I'm ever so fond of that. And we cooked up a wicked spell! One of the best!"

Late news: Lady Macbeth dies in fall from castle battlements. Did she fall, or did she jump? See page 12.

Hail Ross

I have heard. But since Macbeth came to power, things have gone from bad to worse. Why, Lady Macbeth herself has gone mad. Apparently, she keeps thinking that her hands are bloodstained and washes them continually. She wanders the castle all night, wringing them and moaning about the King's murder. If only Macbeth hadn't killed the guards, we might have found out more about why the old King died. I'm not happy. I think there's more to this than meets the eye.

SCOTTISH DAILY NEWS
TROUBLED TIMES
by our military correspondent

It is all over. The tyrant King Macbeth has been defeated in battle and killed by brave Macduff.

Macduff, loyal and true to King Duncan and his family, raised an army against the evil King Macbeth, under whose rule the land has been suffering with the brutal murders of thousands of innocent people.

Heroic General Macduff showed his leadership in battle today when he ordered all the soldiers in his army to cut the boughs off trees in the nearby forest and use them for camouflage. It looked almost as if Birnam Wood was coming to Dunsinane Hill.

Once he had slain devious Macbeth, the valiant General cut off his head and brought it to upstanding Prince Malcolm, son of King Duncan, and the true King of Scotland. Macduff and the fine young prince had joined forces to fight the mad Macbeth, united in the cause to restore rightful reign to our beloved land.

LONG LIVE KING MALCOLM!

General Macduff, who today killed the tyrant King Macbeth. Macbeth recently murdered Macduff's innocent wife and children.

Trivia titbit: Did you know that Macduff's life was saved when he was a newborn baby by being delivered by Caesarean – a way of delivering babies first used at the birth of the late, great Julius Caesar!

Plays are divided into 'acts' and 'scenes'. Here is an extract from Shakespeare's play *Macbeth*, showing a scene where Macbeth meets the witches.

Macbeth: Act 4, Scene 1
by William Shakespeare
Act 4, Scene 1

A cavern. In the middle, a boiling cauldron.
Thunder. Enter the three Witches

First Witch: Thrice the brinded cat hath mew'd.

Second Witch: Thrice, and once the hedge-pig whined.

Third Witch: Harpier cries 'Tis time, 'tis time!

First Witch: Round about the cauldron go;
In the poisoned entrails throw.
Toad, that under cold stone
Days and nights has thirty-one
Swelter'd venom sleeping got,
Boil thou first i' the charmed pot.

All the Witches: Double, double, toil and trouble;
Fire burn, and cauldron bubble.

Second Witch: Fillet of a fenny snake,
In the cauldron boil and bake;
Eye of newt and toe of frog,
Wool of bat and tongue of dog,
Adder's fork and blind-worm's sting,
Lizard's leg and owlet's wing,
For a charm of powerful trouble,
Like a hell-broth boil and bubble.

All: Double, double, toil and trouble;
　　　Fire burn, and cauldron bubble.

Third Witch: Scale of dragon, tooth of wolf,
　　　Witches' mummy, maw and gulf
　　　Of the ravin'd salt-sea shark,
　　　Root of hemlock digg'd i' the dark,
　　　Ditch-deliver'd by a drab,
　　　Make the gruel thick and slab:
　　　Add thereto a tiger's chaudron,
　　　For the ingredients of our cauldron.

All: Double, double, toil and trouble;
　　　Fire burn, and cauldron bubble.

Second Witch: Cool it with a baboon's blood,
　　　Then the charm is firm and good.

Second Witch: By the pricking of my thumbs,
　　　Something wicked this way comes.
　　　Open, locks,
　　　Whoever knocks!

Enter Macbeth

Macbeth: How now, you secret, black, and midnight hags!
　　　What is't you do?

All the Witches: A deed without a name.

Samuel Pepys 1633–1703

Born 17 years after Shakespeare died, Samuel Pepys was a 17th-century English civil servant who is most famous for writing a diary. Pepys recorded his daily life in detail for almost ten years. His diary reveals his jealousies and worries. It is also an important eyewitness account of London in the 1660s, including the Great Plague of 1665, the Great Fire of London in 1666 and the arrival of the Dutch fleet in 1667.

'Pepys' is pronounced 'peeps', although his modern relatives pronounce their name 'pep-iss'.

Pepys's life

Pepys was born in London. On 1st January 1660 he started his diary. In May 1669, he suddenly stopped writing his diary because he was afraid he was losing his sight and his wife died.

When Pepys died, his diaries were left to Magdalene College, Cambridge, where he had been educated. The six volumes were written in a cipher (a disguised way of writing) based on shorthand. The books were first deciphered by John Smith in 1825. The complete diary of more than 3800 pages appeared in 1893.

Samuel Pepys

Pepys's diary

January 1st 1660 Lord's day

This morning (we living lately in the garret,) I rose, put on my suit with great skirts, having not lately worn any other clothes but them. Went to Mr Gunning's chapel at Exeter House, where he made a very good sermon upon these words — 'That in the fulness of time God sent his Son, made of a woman, &c'. Dined at home in the garret, where my wife dressed the remains of a turkey, and in the doing of it she burned her hand. I staid at home the whole afternoon, looking over my accounts, then went with my wife to my father's.

February 25th 1662

Great talk of the effects of this late great wind; and I heard one say that he had five great trees standing together blown down; and, beginning to lop them, one of them, as soon as the lops were cut off, did, by the weight of the root, rise again and fasten. We have letters from the forest of Deane, that above an thousand oakes and as many beeches are blown down in one walke there. And letters from my father tell me of £20 hurt done to us at Brampton.

March 1st 1662

To the Opera, and there saw Romeo and Juliet, the first time it was ever acted. I am resolved to go no more to see the first time of acting, for they were all of them out more or less.

August 27th 1664

All the news this day is, that the Dutch are, with twenty-two sail of ships of warr, crewsing up and down about Ostend: at which we are alarmed. My Lord Sandwich is come back into the Downes with only eight sail, which is or may be a prey to the Dutch, if they knew our weakness and inability to set out any more speedily.

December 31st 1665

Thus ends this year. It is true we have gone through great melancholy because of the great plague. But now the plague is abated almost to nothing, and I entending to get to London as fast as I can, my family, that is, my wife and maids, having been there these two or three weeks. The Dutch war goes on very ill, by reason of lack of money.

My whole family hath been well all this while. But many of such as I know very well, dead. Yet to our great joy, the town fills apace, and shops begin to open again. Pray God continue the plague's decrease.

Pepys often ended his diary entries with the words, 'And so to bed.'

27

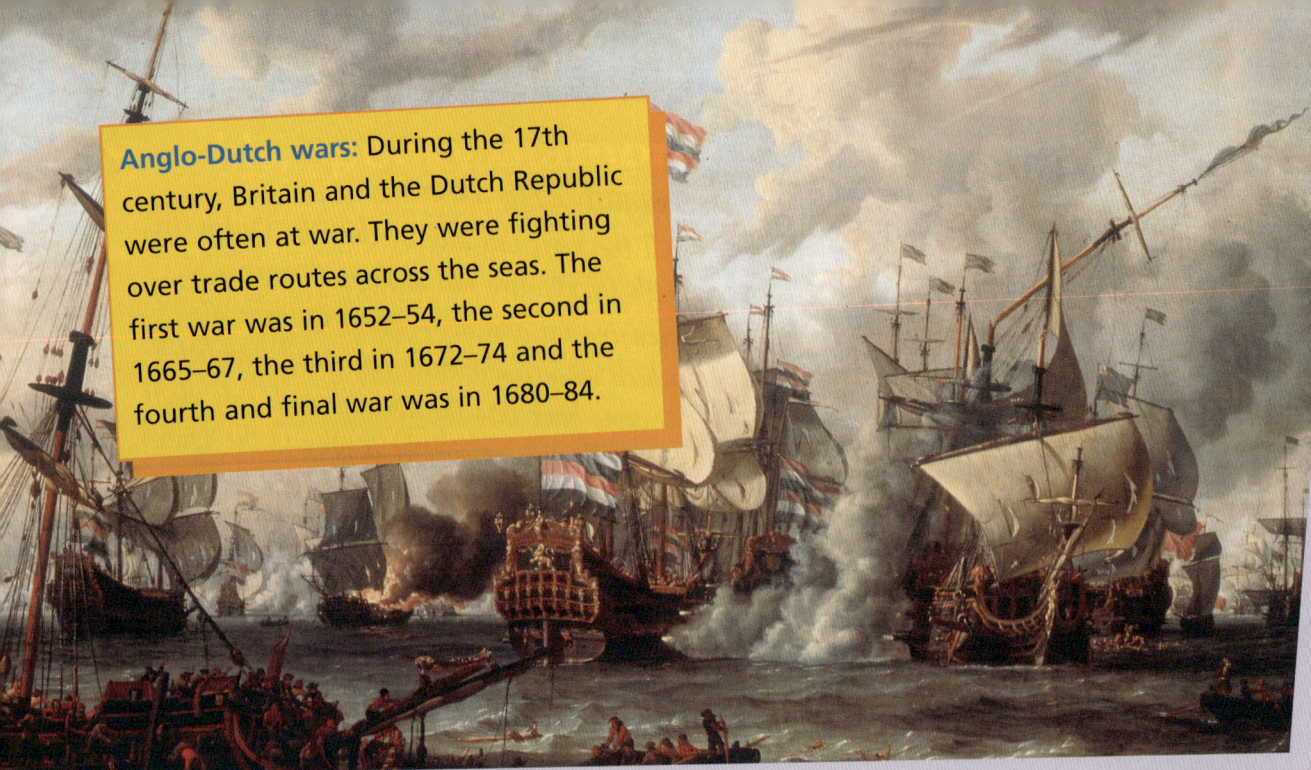

Anglo-Dutch wars: During the 17th century, Britain and the Dutch Republic were often at war. They were fighting over trade routes across the seas. The first war was in 1652–54, the second in 1665–67, the third in 1672–74 and the fourth and final war was in 1680–84.

Pepys's obituary

May 26th 1703

This day died Mr. Sam Pepys, a very worthy, industrious, and curious person, none in England exceeding him in knowledge of the navy, in which he had passed thro' all the most considerable offices, Clerk of the Acts and Secretary of the Admiralty, all which he performed with great integrity. When K. James II. went out of England, he laid down his office, and would serve no more, but withdrawing himselfe from all public affaires, he liv'd at Clapham … where he enjoy'd the fruits of his labours in great prosperity.

He was universally belov'd, hospitable, generous, learned in many things, skilfd in music, a very greate cherisher of learned me... whom he had the conversation.

An obituary is a notice about a person's death. Obituaries often appear in newspapers and give an account of the dead person.

Another diary writer, John Evelyn, wrote about Pepys's death in his diary.

Mr. Pepys had been for neere 40 yeeres my particular friend that Mr. Jackson sent me compleat mourning, desiring me to be one to hold up the pall [help carry the coffin] at his magnificent obsequies, but my indisposition hinder'd me from doing him this last office.

The Great Plague 1665–1671

In 1665, the Great Plague swept through London, killing a quarter of the people who lived there.

Once people were infected, the disease spread quickly. Plague victims would vomit, their tongues would swell, they would have agonising headaches, and huge patches of black skin would appear, along with swollen glands or 'buboes' in the groin and armpits (which is how the names 'Black Death' and 'bubonic plague' came about).

Bubonic plague has been described as one of the most dangerous diseases known to mankind, and has killed more people than any wars ever fought on this planet.

The plague was carried by infected rat fleas and spread through poor and dirty living conditions, particularly in London. The plague was also passed on by infected people sneezing. Many people fled London to escape the plague, but if they were already infected, it meant that the plague spread to the new places they moved to.

The plague stopped in England after 1671. No one knows why, although it might have been that rats and humans had become immune. Also, houses and streets were cleaner, so rats – and their fleas – might not have been able to breed so easily. The Great Fire of London in 1666 also helped by killing lots of rats.

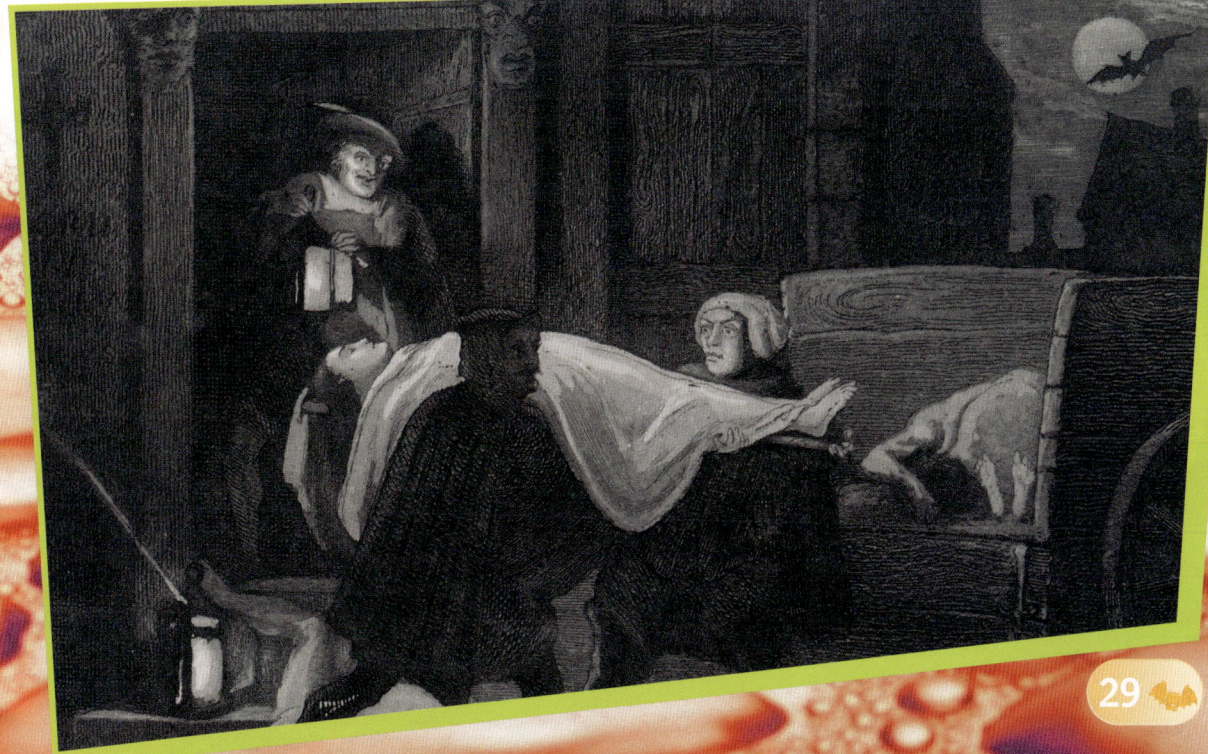

Eyewitness accounts of the Great Plague give us some idea what it was like

A Journal of the Plague Year: a novel by Daniel Defoe

Daniel Defoe wrote a novel that was an account of the Great Plague that he had witnessed.

... the fury of the contagion was such at some particular times, and people sickened so fast and died so soon, that it was impossible, and indeed to no purpose, to go about to inquire who was sick and who was well, or to shut them up with such exactness as the thing required, almost every house in a whole street being infected, and in many places every person in some of the houses; and that which was still worse, by the time that the houses were known to be infected, most of the persons infected would be stone dead, and the rest run away for fear of being shut up.

Bells were used to warn people to stay away from infectious plague corpses.

Plague houses were often boarded shut to stop infection spreading. Sometimes people were still alive inside.

Old women were paid to examine dead bodies to find out whether they were victims of the plague. These women, known as searchers, carried tall white sticks to warn people to stay away from them.

Plague pits

When people died of the plague, they were buried in huge pits as quickly as possible. There are reports that some people were buried before they were actually dead, because others were scared that the 'poisonous smell' from dead plague bodies spread the disease even more quickly than living infected people did.

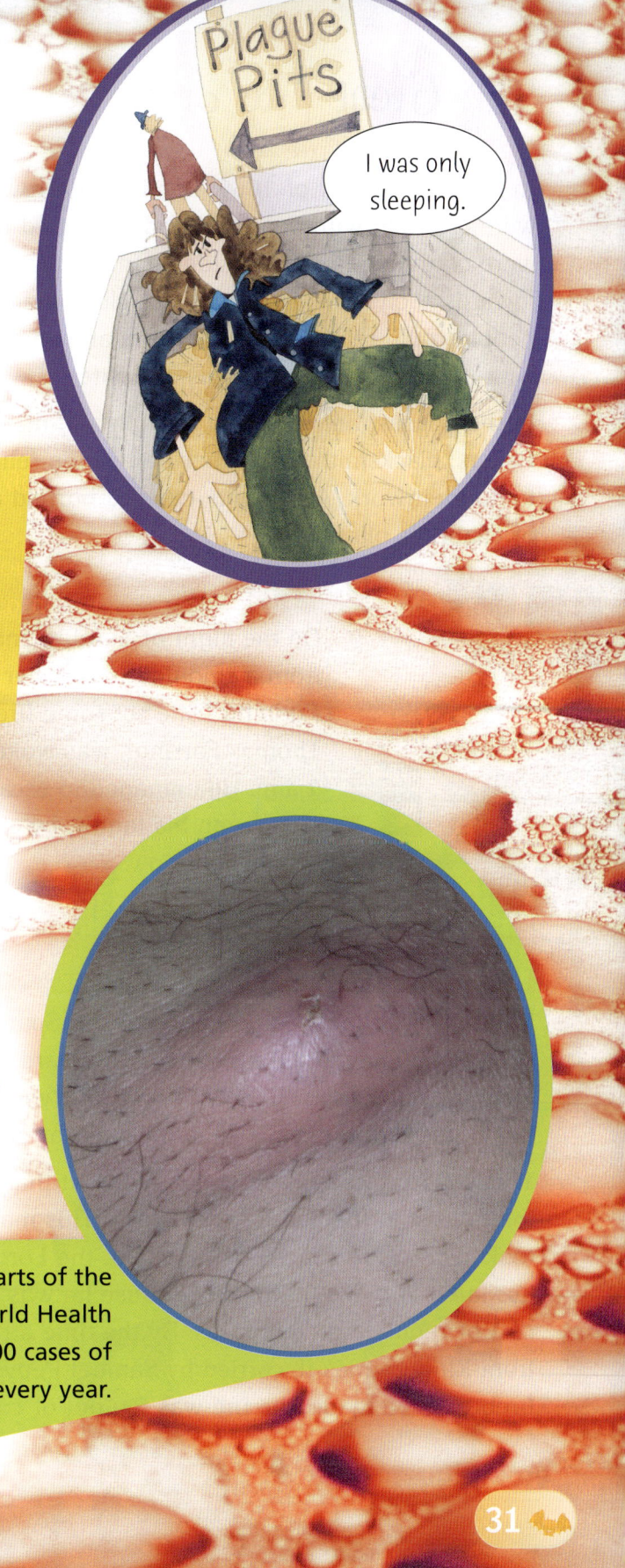

I was only sleeping.

'Ring o' Roses' nursery rhyme

Ring-a-ring o' roses,
A pocket full of posies,
A-tishoo! A-tishoo!
We all fall down.

This rhyme is thought to be about the plague. The 'ring of roses' was the common pattern of buboes (swellings on the body) in the early stage of infections. The 'posies' were flowers, which were thought to ward off infection by sweetening the poisonous plague-filled air. The third line refers to sneezing, which was another early symptom. The last line refers to dying, which is what usually happened next.

The plague still exists in some parts of the world today. The World Health Organization reports 1000–3000 cases of plague every year.

The Great Fire of London 1666

Before the fire

In the hot summer of 1666, London's narrow streets were crowded with people. Wooden-framed buildings were crammed in side by side, leaning over the road towards each other, sometimes so close together that people could reach out of windows and shake hands with the people in the houses opposite.

In the houses, fire was used to cook and make light. Bakers, blacksmiths and other tradesmen relied on fire to do their work. All around, candles burned and wood or coal fires blazed.

Fire!

It'll be toast for breakfast.

On the night of Sunday 2nd September 1666, a spark from a smouldering ember in a baker's oven in Pudding Lane set some firewood on fire. The baker, Thomas Farrinor, was woken by the fire at around 1 a.m. He managed to escape the burning building, along with his family, by climbing out through an upstairs window.

London's burning

It didn't take long for the fire to spread. Sparks from the baker's shop fell on hay in the nearby Star Inn yard, before a strong wind blew the flames to warehouses and wharves filled with food, hemp, oil, hay, timber, coal, spirits and tar on Thames Street.

The way to stop a fire from spreading at that time was to destroy the houses in the path of the flames. This made 'firebreaks' which took away a fire's fuel. On this night, the Lord Mayor of London hesitated to make firebreaks because he was worried about the cost of rebuilding the houses. By the time a royal command came from King Charles II, carried by Samuel Pepys, insisting that firebreaks be made, the fire was too out of control to stop.

The fire had the beneficial effect of killing many of the rats that were responsible for the spread of the Great Plague.

Eyewitness accounts tell us what the Great Fire was like.

John Evelyn's diary entry, 3rd September 1666

Oh the miserable and calamitous spectacle! All the sky was of a fiery aspect, like the top of a burning oven, and the light seen above 40 miles round about for many nights. God grant mine eyes may never behold the like, who now saw above 10,000 houses all in one flame; the noise and cracking and thunder of people, the fall of towers, houses, and churches, was like an hideous storm, and the air all about so hot and inflamed that at last one was not able to approach it, so that they were forced to stand still and let the flames burn on ...

All hands to the pump?

Once the fire had taken hold, the firefighting equipment (wooden ladders, leather buckets, hand-squirts) was no match for the blaze.

King Charles himself took charge of firefighting in parts of the city. He organised lines of men to pass buckets of water from hand to hand from the River Thames to the fire.

The damage

During three days of raging flames, the fire destroyed 13,200 houses, 87 churches (among them St Paul's Cathedral) and 400 streets. Amazingly, fewer than 16 people died in the fire. Most people managed to escape to the fields surrounding the city, where they camped in tents and huts they made.

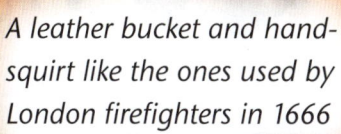

A leather bucket and hand-squirt like the ones used by London firefighters in 1666

Carbon Copy

Introduction

Q: What is the difference between me and a lump of coal?

A: Not much

All plants, creatures and people on Earth are made of carbon. If you sucked all the water out of a person, half of what was left would be carbon. It is in the food we eat, the clothes we wear, the petrol we put in our cars.

We're all made of carbon— even me!

Carbon casebook

Scientists believe that carbon was around before the Earth was created. They say that the universe expanded and then cooled too quickly for carbon to have been made during the Big Bang. They say carbon is made in the interior of stars.

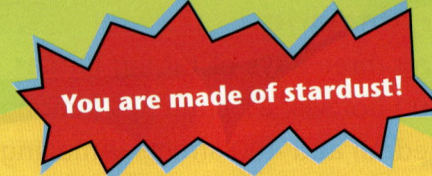
You are made of stardust!

What do all these things have in common?

Did you know ...?

◈ When you have a barbecue, the charcoal that you light is made of carbon.

◈ When you write with a pencil, you are using graphite, which is a kind of carbon.

◈ When you are riding in a car, graphite in oil helps all the engine parts to move smoothly together without sticking.

◈ When you burn your toast, that black stuff is carbon.

The carbon cycle

Millions of years ago, trees died and then, over time, turned into coal and oil and gas. We call them fossil fuels because they are made of fossilised trees and animals, but their main ingredient is carbon.

Even diamonds, some of the Earth's most precious gems, are a transparent form of pure carbon. Funnily enough, diamond is one of the hardest things on Earth and graphite is one of the softest. But they are both made of carbon. Diamonds are used in jewellery but they are also used as drill bits because they are so hard. Graphite and charcoal are used for drawing.

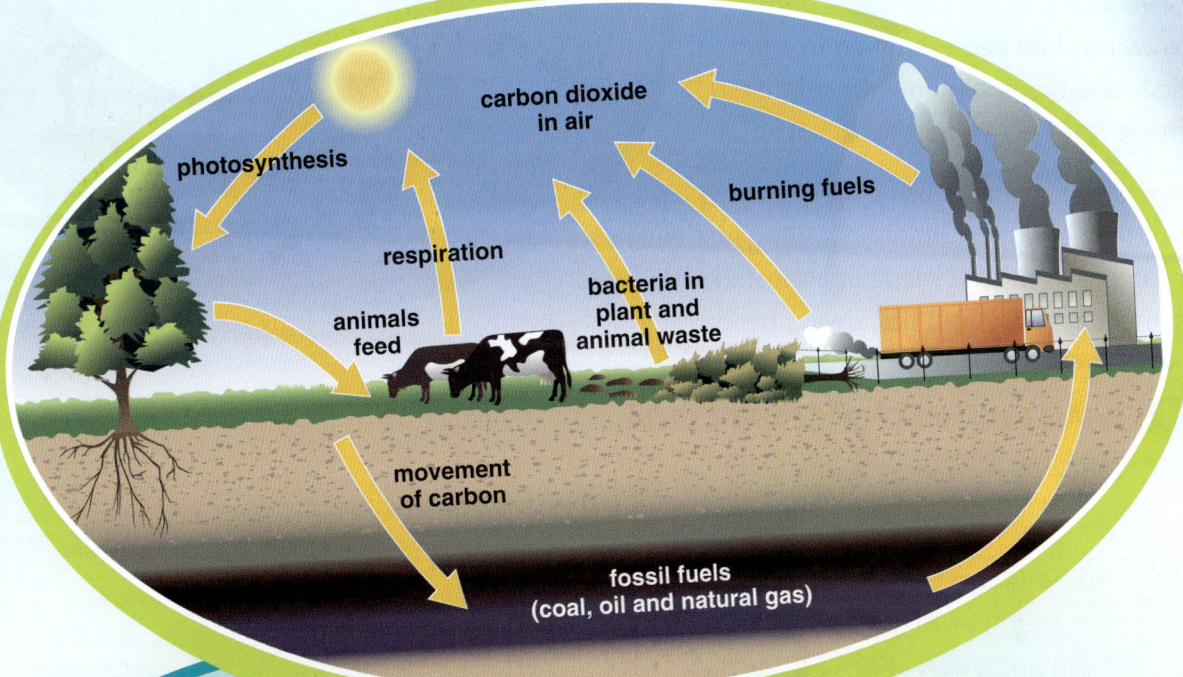

carbon dioxide
in air

photosynthesis

burning fuels

respiration

bacteria in
plant and
animal waste

animals
feed

movement
of carbon

fossil fuels
(coal, oil and natural gas)

The word carbon comes from the Latin 'carbo', meaning charcoal, which has been known to man since fire was discovered. Charcoal is a very good fuel because it gives out twice as much heat as wood does. Early Britons used the heat from charcoal to make bronze and iron. The Egyptians used it to make copper and the Romans used it to make glass.

Charcoal — then and now

Secret hobby of cavemen

Cavemen living 30,000 years ago had a very simple, hard life compared with us. But they had hobbies, just like us, and one of them was drawing.

Scientists who investigated a cave in France, near Marseille, found beautiful drawings of horses, seals and fish that were 27,000 years old. Some of the drawings had been outlined in charcoal first, and then painted with colours made from plants and earth.

Nowadays, painters use better quality paint, but they often still draw their work first with charcoal — which is made in almost exactly the same way today as it has always been.

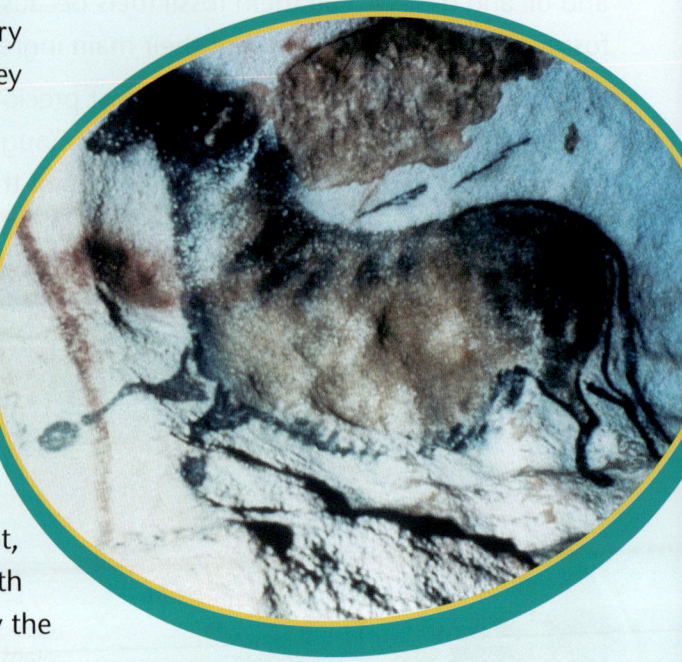

Drawing with charcoal

Did you know ...?

- ◈ You can use charcoal and graphite (the lead in pencils) together in drawing.
- ◈ Charcoal is good for drawing rough things like wood, bark, fur, hair, eyelashes, leather and shadows.
- ◈ Graphite is good for shading in skin, glass, china and metal in drawings, and for drawing smooth fabrics like silk.
- ◈ You can get really good effects in a picture by blending charcoal lines — lightly rubbing over what you have drawn. Try using tissue or small felt squares for this. If you use your fingers, the natural oils in your skin will make your finished work look shiny, and it's easy to mess up the rest of your work.

Charcoal and gunpowder

Charcoal is used to make gunpowder, also called black powder. Gunpowder is used to propel bullets and fireworks. It was invented by the Chinese around the 8th century AD. John Evelyn, the diarist, whose family was licensed to make gunpowder for the King, wrote in 1664: 'There is made of charcoal usually three sorts, viz. one for the iron-works, a second for gunpowder, and a third for London and the Court.'

viz. (from the Latin *videlicet*) = 'that is to say', 'in other words'

Charcoal was cool with cavemen, and it's great for gunpowder too!

Making charcoal

There is a big tradition of making charcoal – called charcoal burning – in Britain.

Charcoal burners make a special kiln out of earth and fill it with wood. The secret of making good charcoal is to burn it very slowly over two to three days. The kiln has to be constantly watched.

Because wood is needed to make charcoal, many trees are being cut down. Huge mangrove forests in some countries, such as Indonesia, are disappearing and the charcoal made there is often shipped all around the world. Not only does this damage the countries that are losing the forests, but it damages the seas too.

Conservationists would like more charcoal to be produced in the UK. This would help to save tropical rainforests, preserve woodland species of insects and butterflies in the UK, and reduce the amount of pollution caused by transporting charcoal.

If you burn a match, the tip of the wood turns to charcoal. This is called an irreversible change, because you can't turn it back to wood. Once cavemen had discovered fire, they found out about charcoal.

Are we burning dead dinosaurs?

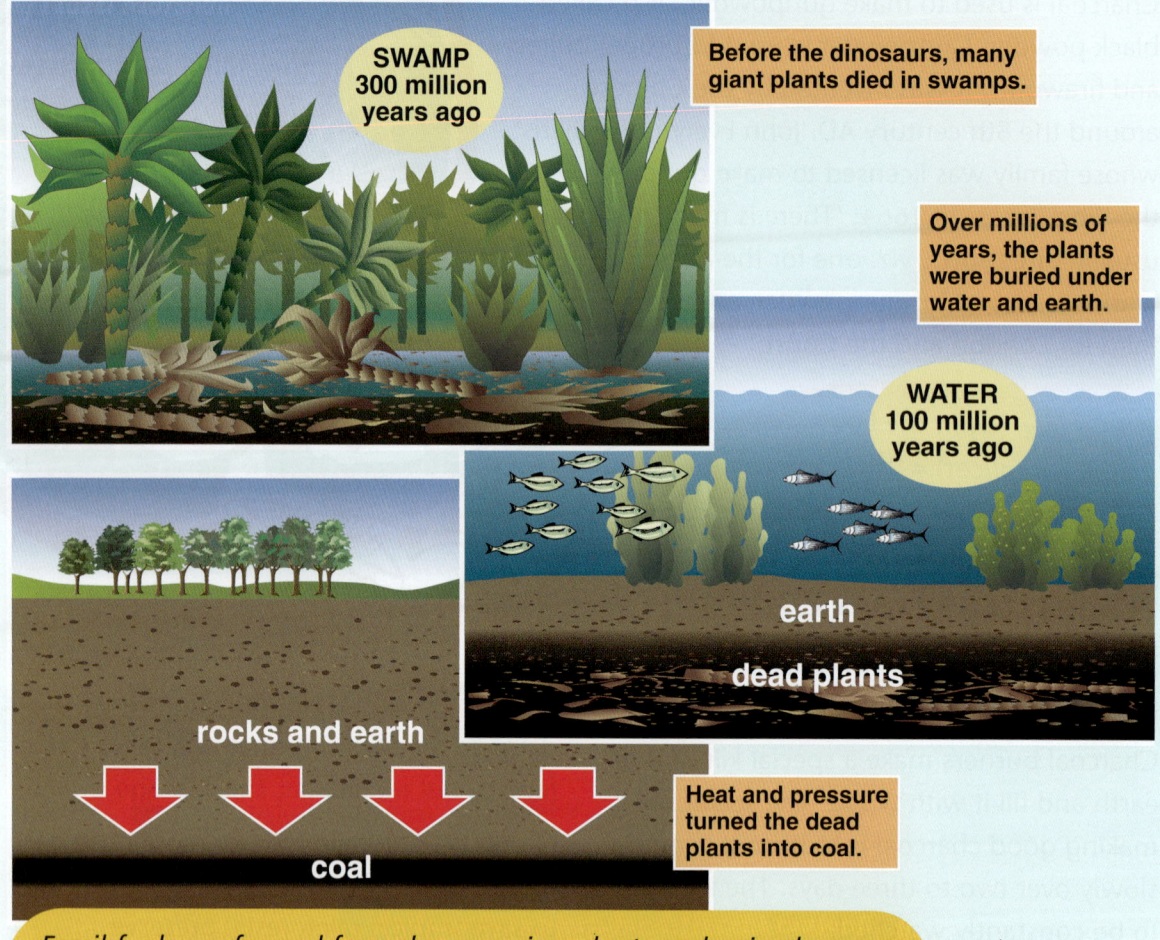

**SWAMP
300 million
years ago**

Before the dinosaurs, many giant plants died in swamps.

Over millions of years, the plants were buried under water and earth.

**WATER
100 million
years ago**

earth

dead plants

rocks and earth

Heat and pressure turned the dead plants into coal.

coal

*Fossil fuels are formed from decomposing plants and animals.
When plants and animals decompose, most of what is left is carbon.*

We call coal, oil and gas fossil fuels. Lots of people think this means they must be made of dead dinosaurs. In fact, most of the fossil fuels we find today were formed millions of years before the first dinosaurs.

Fossil fuels are formed from plants and animals that lived 300 million years ago in swamps and oceans. At that time, the land masses we live on today were just forming. There were swamps and bogs everywhere, and all had trees and plants growing in them. The climate was warmer. Strange-looking animals walked on the land, and weird-looking fish swam in the rivers and seas. Tiny one-celled organisms called protoplankton floated in the ocean.

When these things died, they sank and rotted away and became buried under layers and layers of mud, rock and sand. Eventually hundreds, and sometimes thousands of metres of earth covered them. In some areas, the decomposing materials were covered by ancient seas, before the seas dried up.

After millions of years, mostly just carbon was left. But the carbon joined with hydrogen, which is a gas, and formed what we know as coal, oil and gas. Chemists call fossil fuels hydrocarbons.

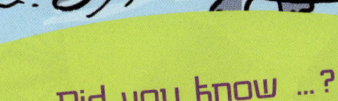

Did you know ...?

⬦ Even today, in some pieces of coal you can find the outlines of ferns and other long-dead plants. About 10m of prehistoric plant debris could be pushed down to make 1m of coal.

⬦ Coal helped the Industrial Revolution. Without it, there would have been no steam power – no trains and no big machines or factories. In 1851, 394,000 people worked in coal mines all over Britain. Now, there are about 10,000 people working in just 11 deep pits.

⬦ Women and children under the age of 13 worked down the mines until a law was passed against this in 1842.

⬦ Ponies were used in mines to pull heavy loads.

Going down.

The origins of oil

What is an oil well?

An oil well is not like a well for water. Oil doesn't exist in deep, black pools. If you looked down an oil well you wouldn't see a big underground lake – oil wells are lots and lots of tiny oil droplets trapped inside rocks. You can only see these droplets through a microscope. The droplets cling to the rock, like drops of water cling to a window pane.

The oil is under pressure, too, because of all the millions of tons of rock lying on it, and from the gases underground. This means that when workers strike oil, the natural pressure is released – like the air escaping from a balloon. Nowadays, oil companies can control this sudden burst, but when people first struck oil they called it a gusher – because it sprayed all over them.

 Is it just a hole full of oil?

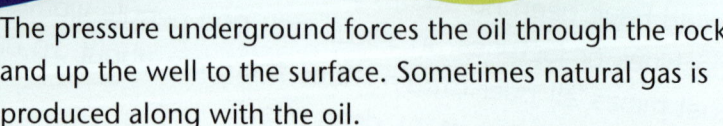

- Oil was discovered in the North Sea in the 1970s.
- There are 55 British oil fields in the North Sea.
- By the time oil production stops in the North Sea it is thought that 55 billion barrels of oil will have been produced.
- One barrel contains 190 litres of crude oil.

I know you're in there.

The pressure underground forces the oil through the rock and up the well to the surface. Sometimes natural gas is produced along with the oil.

Oil companies will start drilling wells only when they are absolutely certain they've found the right kind of rocks. When the pressure underground drops, oil companies use pumps to bring the oil to the surface.

The world's greatest firefighter

Red Adair is probably the world's greatest firefighter – he puts out blazes in oil fields. An oil well on fire can be terrifying and extremely dangerous. Even after you put out the fire, if the oil is still gushing, there is a danger that it will burst into flames again at any moment, so the well also needs to be capped – like turning a tap off. Red Adair has put out around 1000 oil fires around the world, including the Piper Alpha disaster in the North Sea in 1988, and 628 oil well fires in Kuwait after the First Gulf War in 1991.

What do we use oil for?

Crude oil can be turned into more than 4000 different things, including liquefied petroleum gas (LPG), which some people use to heat their homes; petrol; asphalt (used in paving roads); perfumes; insecticides; plastics, synthetic fibres (for making clothes), synthetic rubbers, detergents and chemical fertilisers.

Sometimes the oil tankers transporting oil have accidents at sea, and the cargo of oil spills out onto the water. When this happens, it usually causes great damage to seabirds, fish and the environment.

A fire at an oil well can be extremely dangerous.

Oil slick brings black death

"I used to be a fisherman," says Danny Rodriguez, with an ironic smile, as he scrubs oil off his doorstep. "But we have not been able to take the boats out since the black tide came."

The windows of Danny's house, near the beach, are flecked with fat drops of oil. Tar coats the walkway outside and stains the benches where Danny and his friends meet. Worse still, the rocks below, home to goose barnacles and crabs, are blackened; the creatures that live there are dead. With every black tide comes a carpet of evil sludge, and its froth of drowned birds and fish.

Danny can see his future clearly. "It's black, black, black – like the oil."

41

The dangers of carbon

Human beings are made of carbon. Without it, we couldn't exist, but the way we are using it is threatening our lives and our planet.

Carbon dioxide, which is a mixture of carbon and oxygen, is forming an invisible envelope around our planet. It is acting like a greenhouse under the sun. This means the temperature is rising. The ice caps at the Antarctic and Arctic are melting and making the sea levels rise. People living on some islands in the Pacific Ocean fear their homes might disappear forever underwater.

Pollution and the loss of trees and forests are affecting levels of carbon dioxide in the air.

The level of carbon dioxide in the air has risen by a third since the middle of the 19th century, when the Industrial Revolution began. This happened because, when people realised they could use steam to power factory machines and trains, they burned coal to heat the boilers which made the steam. More machines and more factories all burning fossil fuels released huge amounts of carbon dioxide into the air. Then, cars were invented. Cars burn petrol and oil, which also produces carbon dioxide (and carbon monoxide, which is highly poisonous). Steam power has gone out of fashion, but coal is still burned in power stations to make electricity. Trees take carbon dioxide out of the air but with more trees being cut down, those that are left can't cope with all the carbon dioxide in the atmosphere.

How we can have cleaner, safer power

Lots of countries are now looking at ways of using power that don't harm the Earth.

- More giant wind turbines which create electricity from the wind are being built across Europe.
- Lots of houses and factories now have solar panels on their roofs, which collect energy from the sun's rays.
- Ways of using the power of waves are being looked at.
- More buildings are being built with lots of insulation, so that they don't take so much energy to heat.

In the 1950s, the first nuclear power stations were built in Britain. They were hailed as a clean alternative to coal-powered electricity. However, they are now being closed down because the metals they use remain very dangerous for thousands of years, and nobody knows how to keep them safe for this long.

How you can save energy

- Walk to school if you can, or ask to be dropped off at a distance from school.
- Keep heating and air conditioning turned down.
- Turn off lights, radios and televisions when you go out.
- If you're cold, wear more clothes.

Sparkly, spooky diamonds

Diamonds are the hardest things on Earth – but they are made of carbon, just like graphite, which is one of the softest things.

Nowadays, most diamonds are used in industry as cutting tools. But some diamonds are so sparkly and beautiful that people want to wear them as jewellery. Some diamonds are so beautiful that people have killed to get them.

I'm the hardest thing on Earth.

The Hope Diamond

Once, it seemed that anyone who owned the Hope Diamond would immediately die or have incredibly bad luck. This beautiful blue diamond – a very rare colour for a diamond – is thought to have been part of the French Crown Jewels which were stolen just after King Louis XVI and Queen Marie Antoinette were beheaded during the French Revolution.

Terrible, unlucky things seemed to happen to later owners of the Hope Diamond. Some lost all their money, others killed themselves or were murdered. Then, in 1947, the diamond was put on show and raised nearly £1 million for charity. Now, it is the property of the Smithsonian Institute in Washington, DC, USA.

the Hope Diamond

Healing powers

Diamonds were also once thought to have healing powers. Queen Elizabeth I wore a diamond around her neck to guard against infection. And in 1534, Pope Clement VII became very ill and was given crushed diamonds – worth about £30,000 today – as a medicine to eat. He died anyway.

If you were born in April, your birthstone is diamond.

Diamond facts

Diamonds can only be cut by other diamonds, or by lasers, although they can be shattered or split if hit really hard.

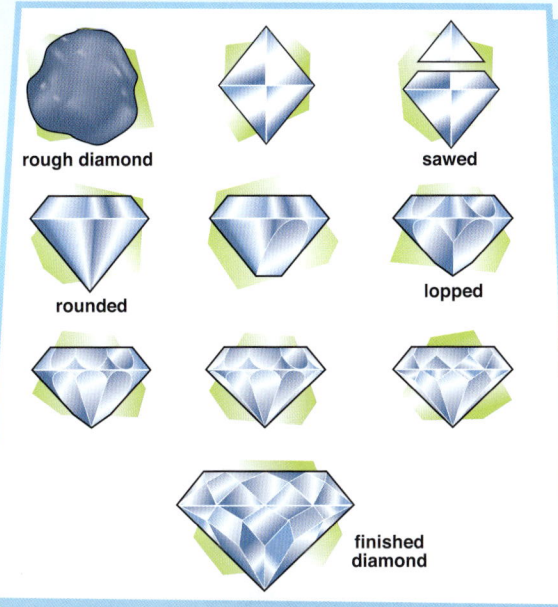

rough diamond

sawed

rounded

lopped

finished diamond

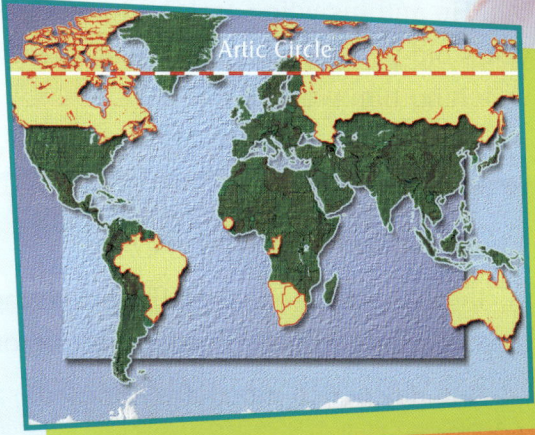

Arctic Circle

Most diamonds are found in South Africa, Namibia, Botswana, the Republic of Congo and Sierra Leone. There are also deposits in Canada, the Russian Arctic, Brazil and in northern and western Australia. Can you find these countries on this map?

How a diamond is cut: rough diamonds often have to be split before they are cut (shaped) and polished. They are cut many times and given faces, called facets, until they are finished. Only then will they look like the sparkly jewels we know.

- Diamonds are weighed in carats. A carat weighs about the same as a small paper clip.
- Lots of people nowadays buy diamond engagement rings – diamonds are so old that De Beers, the company which sells diamonds, uses the slogan, 'a diamond is forever'.
- The biggest diamond in the universe – measuring 4000 km across – has been discovered inside a star. It is 50 light years from Earth and weighs 10 billion trillion trillion carats.

Diamonds are formed deep beneath the Earth's surface under intense heat and pressure. They have come to the Earth's surface during earthquakes or volcanic eruptions.

The Jeweller's Clever Daughter

by Adèle Geras

Jacob the jeweller lived in a small house at the bottom of a steep hill. He and his wife Sarah had one daughter, Esther. She was seven years old and loved to sit on a stool in the corner of her father's shop, watching him work.

Ladies came to him with all sorts of problems.

'The precious stone has fallen out of this ring,' they would say. 'Could you put it back for me?'

Jacob would look carefully at the ring and say, 'Don't worry, my dear. I will do my best. Come for it before the Sabbath next week.'

One day, a rich merchant appeared, and put a fine diamond on Jacob's table.

'I bought this diamond for my daughter's wedding,' he said, 'but it has a mark on it. It's like a line, spoiling the jewel.'

Jacob looked carefully at the diamond and said, 'Don't worry, sir. I will do my best. Come for it before the Sabbath next week.'

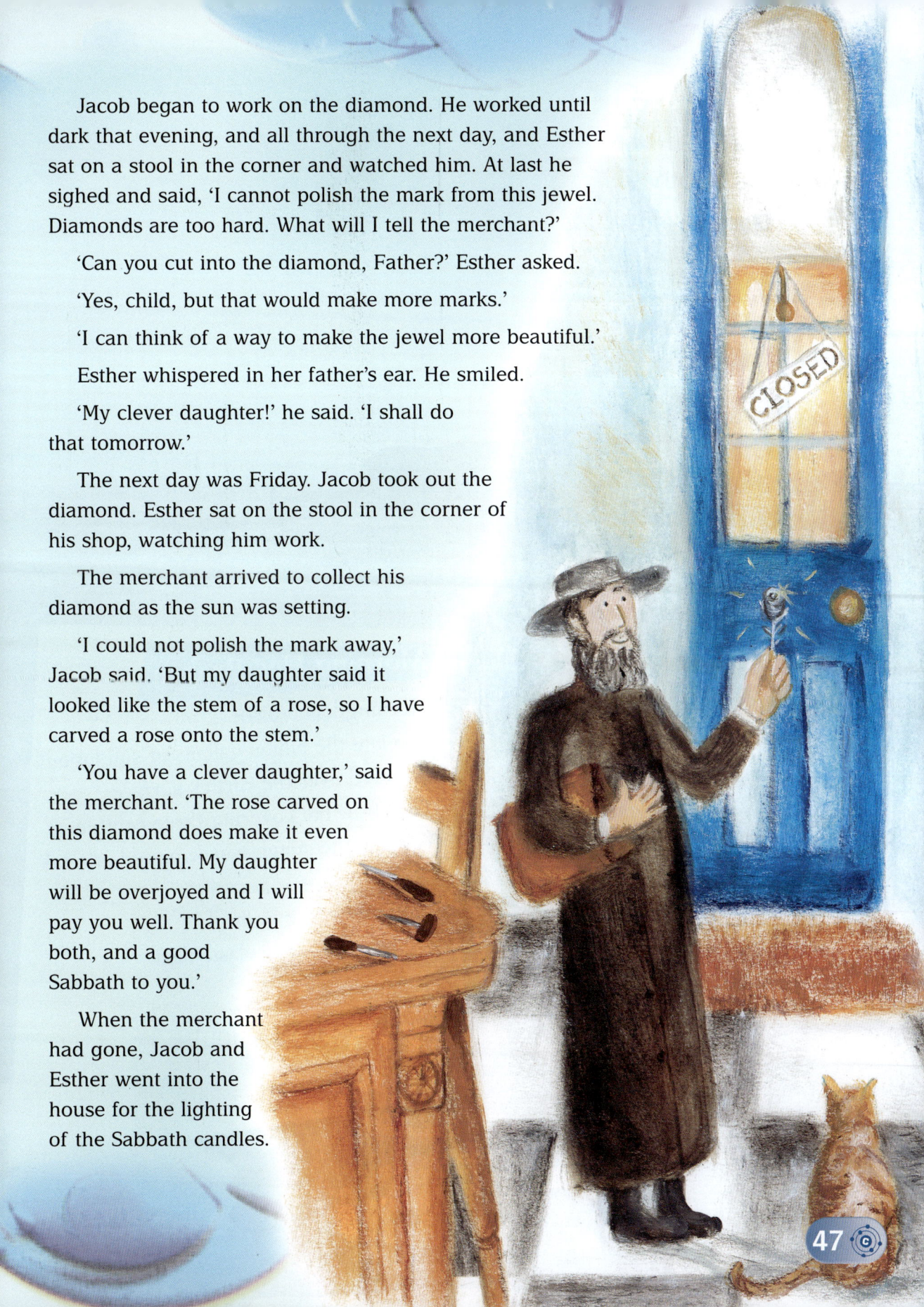

Jacob began to work on the diamond. He worked until dark that evening, and all through the next day, and Esther sat on a stool in the corner and watched him. At last he sighed and said, 'I cannot polish the mark from this jewel. Diamonds are too hard. What will I tell the merchant?'

'Can you cut into the diamond, Father?' Esther asked.

'Yes, child, but that would make more marks.'

'I can think of a way to make the jewel more beautiful.'

Esther whispered in her father's ear. He smiled.

'My clever daughter!' he said. 'I shall do that tomorrow.'

The next day was Friday. Jacob took out the diamond. Esther sat on the stool in the corner of his shop, watching him work.

The merchant arrived to collect his diamond as the sun was setting.

'I could not polish the mark away,' Jacob said. 'But my daughter said it looked like the stem of a rose, so I have carved a rose onto the stem.'

'You have a clever daughter,' said the merchant. 'The rose carved on this diamond does make it even more beautiful. My daughter will be overjoyed and I will pay you well. Thank you both, and a good Sabbath to you.'

When the merchant had gone, Jacob and Esther went into the house for the lighting of the Sabbath candles.

47

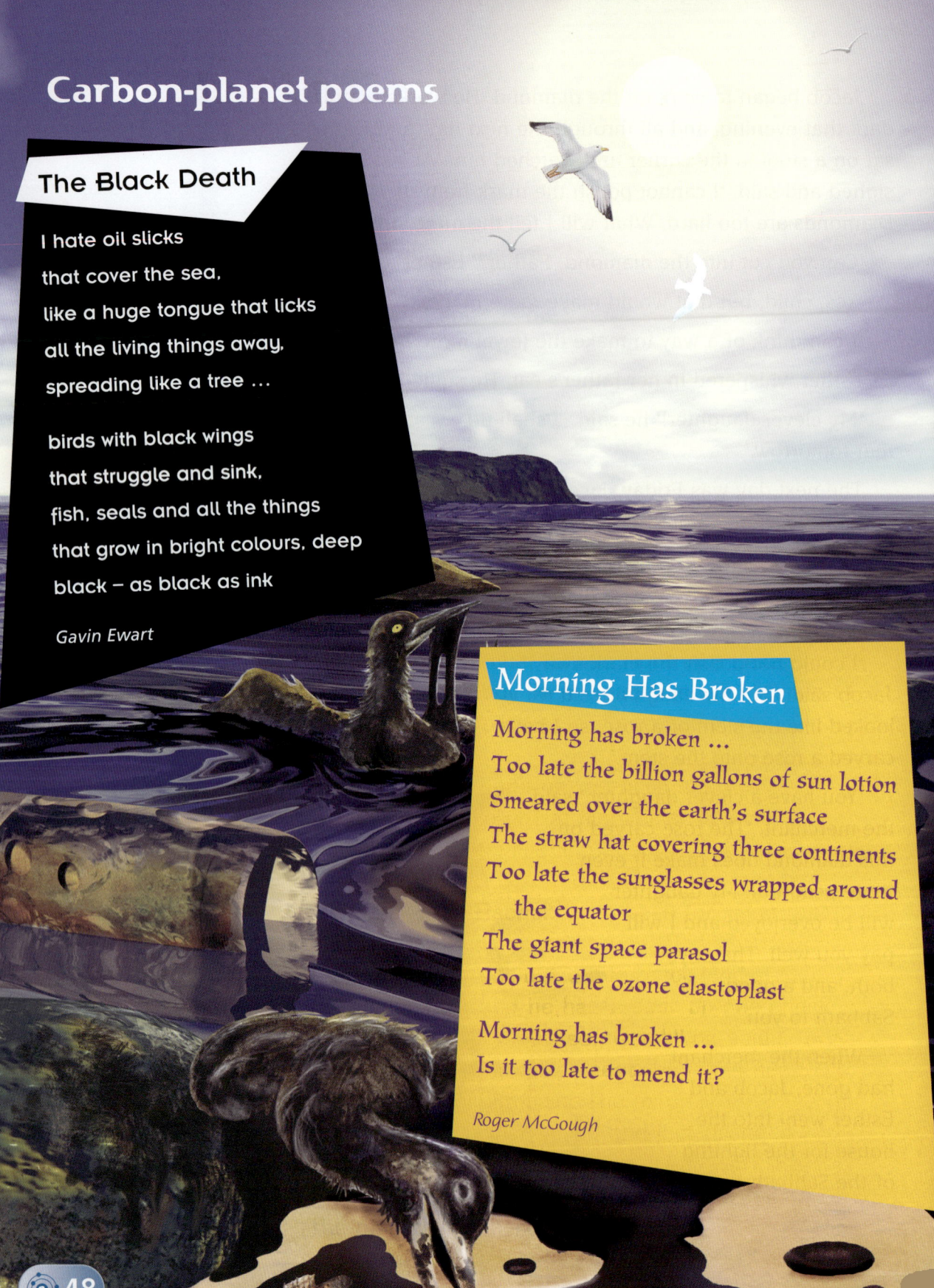

Carbon-planet poems

The Black Death

I hate oil slicks
that cover the sea,
like a huge tongue that licks
all the living things away,
spreading like a tree ...

birds with black wings
that struggle and sink,
fish, seals and all the things
that grow in bright colours, deep
black – as black as ink

Gavin Ewart

Morning Has Broken

Morning has broken ...
Too late the billion gallons of sun lotion
Smeared over the earth's surface
The straw hat covering three continents
Too late the sunglasses wrapped around
the equator
The giant space parasol
Too late the ozone elastoplast

Morning has broken ...
Is it too late to mend it?

Roger McGough

The Way Through the Woods

They shut the road through the woods
Seventy years ago.
Weather and rain have undone it again,
And now you would never know
There was once a road through the woods
Before they planted the trees.
It is underneath the coppice and heath,
And the thin anemones.
Only the keeper sees
That, where the ring-dove broods,
And the badgers roll at ease,
There was once a road through the woods.

Yet, if you enter the woods
Of a summer evening late,
When the night-air cools on the trout-ringed pools
Where the otter whistles his mate,
(They fear not men in the woods,
Because they see so few)
You will hear the beat of a horse's feet
And the swish of a skirt in the dew,
Steadily cantering through
The misty solitudes,
As though they perfectly knew
The old lost road through the woods ...
But there is no road through the woods.

Rudyard Kipling

Landscape

What will you find at the
    edge of the world?
A footprint
a feather,
desert sand swirled?
A tree of ice,
a rain of stars,
or a junkyard of cars?

What will there be at the
    rim of the earth?
A mollusc,
a mammal,
a new creature's birth?
Eternal sunrise,
immortal sleep,
or cars piled up in a rusty heap?

Eve Merriam

The Chase

by Hazel Marshall

'Jamie! Take this! You'll have to run!'

Jamie MacPhail, kitchen lad at Edinburgh Castle, looked confused. The soldier handed him a sealed letter.

'This is urgent,' he said. 'It has to reach the London stagecoach at Holyrood. If you manage, I'll give you a penny.' Jamie gaped with a mix of horror and excitement. It was a full mile to Holyrood, the coach left at one and it was almost that now.

He started to run. He could see Holyrood down the hill and thought he could just get there in time. What he didn't see was Andrew, the castle bully, who wanted to get that penny for himself, setting off after him.

Jamie managed to avoid the contents of a chamber pot thrown from a tenement window, but he tripped over a pig which had strolled nonchalantly from a narrow side wynd. He landed face first in the muddy road and didn't notice Andrew running past him.

Picking himself up, he ran on, past the Tolbooth, wondering what was in the letter. He was sure it was full of important military information.

The wind snatched the letter from his hand and sent it dancing down the street. A large booted foot stopped its headlong flight.

'What's this?'

Jamie groaned. What was Andrew doing here?

'Can I have my letter back?' asked Jamie.

Andrew grinned and ran off. Jamie gave chase. At least Andrew was heading in the right direction! But how was he to get the letter back?

At the Tron, a coach had stopped at the diggings of the new bridge. The lord inside wanted to watch, and so his men were stopping everyone getting past. Andrew was caught by the lord's men as he tried to pass.

Seeing his chance, Jamie snatched the letter from Andrew's hand and dashed under the stationary coach.

He was over halfway now. Looking over his shoulder he could see that Andrew had got away and was chasing him again.

'Whoa there!'

He was grabbed by the keeper of the Netherbow toll gate.

'Where are you going in such a hurry?'

'I have to deliver this letter to the stagecoach,' he panted out. He could see that Andrew was gaining on him.

The keeper looked from Jamie to the stagecoach where the men were shutting the doors and laughed.

'You'd better run faster then.'

Jamie looked over his shoulder and saw that Andrew was almost upon him.

'That boy says that gatekeepers are too slow to catch anyone,' he said.

'Oh, does he?' said the gatekeeper grimly. 'We'll see about that.'

Jamie ran towards the stagecoach. He could see that the doors were shut, the luggage was piled on top and the driver was raising his whip, ready to start the horses.

Jamie arrived in time to grab one of the horse's reins.

'What are you doing?' shouted the driver.

'I have an urgent letter for one of your passengers,' gasped Jamie.

'Be quick about it,' said the driver. 'I've a long way to go.'

'Letter for Cameron!' Jamie shouted.

'That's me,' said a female voice, and a gloved hand reached out for it.

Jamie handed it over and was thrilled when he was given a penny in return.

The coach drove off.

Jamie looked at the penny and thought for a moment about the important information he thought he had carried all the way down the Royal Mile. He hadn't known it was only a love letter that was so important. As he walked back up the street he smiled and waved at Andrew who was still being held by the Netherbow gatekeeper. By the time Andrew got back to the castle Jamie would have hidden his two pennies.

The Mayan Man of Gold

retold by Chris Buckton

Very long ago there were four gods. They created a wonderful earth, full of plants and animals, and a sea teeming with fish. But one thing was missing. The gods wanted someone to worship them and to appreciate the beauty of the world. They decided to create a human being.

At first, they used clay to model the figure, but when it rained, the body dissolved and crumbled. Then, they tried wood, but it burned too easily in the fire. Last, they tried gold. The figure didn't melt in fire and it wasn't harmed by water. The gods were satisfied. 'Now he can praise us,' they said.

But the gold man did nothing. He just stared into space and didn't speak.

So the fourth god decided to try flesh. He took out his knife and cut off his own fingers.

The fingers scuttled away across the earth and became fingermen, the first people. They busied about, finding out about the world and cultivating the earth.

One day, the fingermen found the gold man. They expected him to speak or move, and they were puzzled when he did nothing. They touched him gently and found that he was very cold. 'Perhaps he's ill,' they thought, so they wrapped him in a cloak and carried him with them on their travels. They looked after him tenderly, as if he was alive. After a while, the gold man became warm, and at last his heart began to beat, and he spoke the words of praise that the gods had waited for.

The gods were overjoyed. The gold man had been brought to life by the kindness and care of the fingermen. The gods wished to reward the people they had created. From that day on, the man of gold and all his descendants were wealthy, and repaid the fingermen's kindness by looking after them. And no gold man could enter heaven without a fingerman taking him there.

Isaiah, Chapter 46

Some pour out gold from their bags
  and weigh out silver on the scales;
They hire a goldsmith to make it into a god,
  and they bow down and worship it.
They lift it to their shoulders and carry it;
  they set it up in its place, and there it stands.
From that spot it cannot move.
Though one cries out to it, it does not answer;
  it cannot save him from his troubles.

The Bible

The Great Cake Disaster

by Chris Buckton

My friend Ann and I had been sent to the baker's to buy a double-layer cream cake for her mother's posh tea party. We weren't invited.

The cream cakes tempted us, sitting there in the shop window with their oozing jam and cream. It was unbearable.

I had an inspiration. We had enough money to buy a triple-layer cake. We scrambled up the railway embankment, opened the cake box and gulped with greed. I took off the bottom layer, pudgy and powdery, and divided it in two. We stuffed it in our mouths.

'Now put the rest back in the box,' I told Ann, 'and your mum will never know.'

Ann stopped halfway. 'It's all jammy.'

Oh no! I shouldn't have taken the bottom layer, it should have been the middle. That way it wouldn't have shown at all. Idiot, idiot …

'Put some earth on the jammy bit. We'll tell her that we dropped it.'

We rehearsed our story. But Ann's mum didn't even open the box. She asked us to arrange it on a doily.

The posh friends arrived for the posh tea party. Ann and I sat in the kitchen, giggling and hoping for the best. But the best didn't happen. Ann's mother stood at the kitchen door with the sponge cake.

'Can you explain this?' She pointed with her long red fingernail and prodded at the mud and jam.

Yes, we could explain it. Two rough boys had attacked us. They'd tried to take the cake, we had bravely saved the cake, but in the struggle, we'd dropped the cake …

'I see. Where's my change?'

We'd never thought of that.

Ann told her mother that I'd made her do it. What a scumbag. When my father got to hear about it he told me a poem. I've never forgotten it.

Oh what a tangled web we weave
When first we practise to deceive.

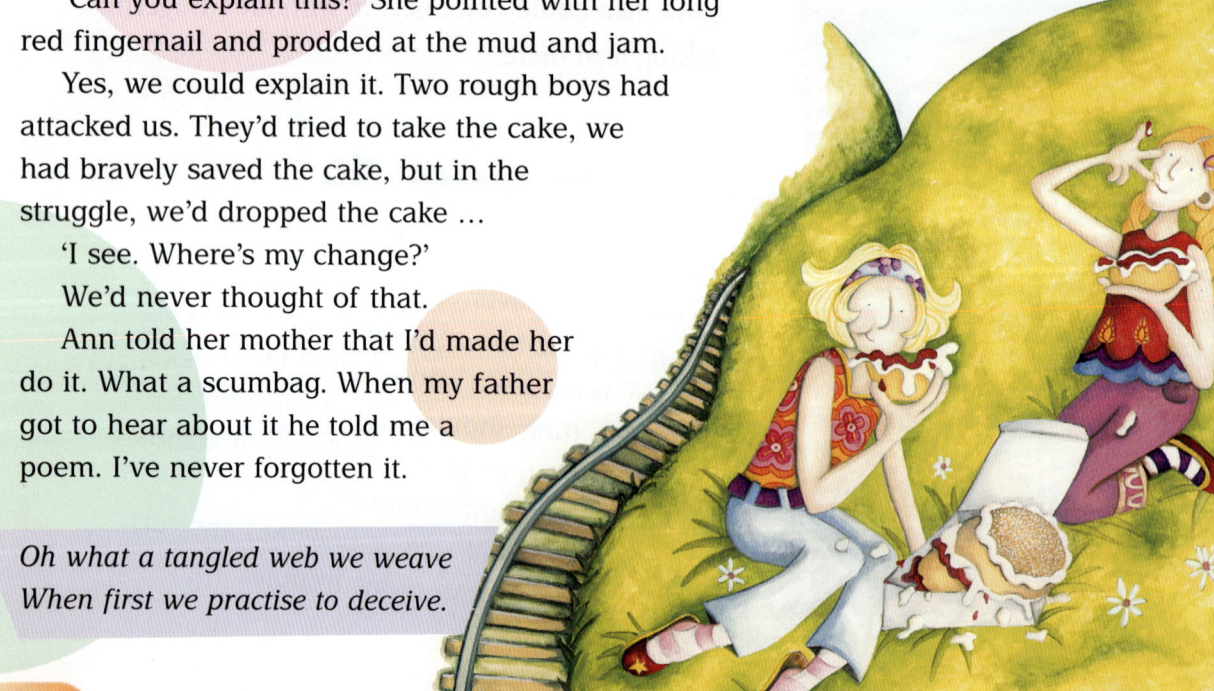

56

The Fallen Angel Cake

by Maggie Pearson

I'm not saying my mum's a bad cook. But the angel cake she baked for the cake stall at the village fête was a disaster. It looked like the cat had sat on it.

'If I turn it upside down,' she said, 'and ice it, the dent in the middle won't show.'

She turned it upside down – and the middle fell out.

'Don't cry,' I said. 'We can fill up the hole with something round and not too heavy –'

'Like what?' she said.

'Like a toilet roll! Cover the lot over with icing. And I'll nip down to the fête as soon as it opens and buy it back!'

So that's what we did.

Except I couldn't buy it back. Mum's cake wasn't on the cake stall.

We spent the whole afternoon trying to find out what had happened to it. We were still there when it came to the clearing up. So we helped with that. Then Chloe's mum invited us back to her place.

I knew how it would be: tea in bone china cups, funny little forks to eat the cake with, and having to take our shoes off so as not to mark the carpet.

It was worse than that. Much worse.

Right in the middle of the table sat my mum's cake!

We were getting up the courage to confess when someone said, 'Oh! What a beautiful cake!'

Chloe's mum beamed. 'Thank you,' she said. 'I baked it myself.'

In the Back Seat

by Kevin Crossley-Holland

Abby's my best friend and this happened to her sister, and Abby told me about it, so I know it's true.

Her sister's 18 and she's got a car, and she's called Rachel. Last week, well, she went to a late night party. Somewhere in town, I don't know where exactly, and it ended very late. About two o'clock.

By the time Rachel drove home, the city was all empty. That's spooky! Anyhow, Rachel got going and she looked in the mirror, and there was this truck kind-of-thing, right behind her. She could see the driver, and he was big and leaning forward and well ... he started flashing her: headlights, dipped lights, no lights. No lights in the dark, that's really dangerous. Well, the man kept flashing her and Rachel didn't know what to do. She just drove as fast as she could. But when she turned left, the man turned left. Then Rachel turned right into Lake Street – that's where Abby lives – and this man turned right as well. He even followed her into her own driveway.

Rachel just put her hand on the horn and never took it off. In the middle of the night. Her dad woke straight up and he came rushing down to find out what was going on.

'That man!' cried Rachel. 'He's been following me and flashing me right across town.'

Then the driver got out of his truck kind-of-thing. He was big and he had a scar on one cheek – you could see the stitches. 'Quick!' he said. 'There's a man in her back seat. I flashed her every time I saw him raise the axe.'

Then Abby's father yelled and just dragged Rachel out of the car. And the driver with the scar, he ripped open the back door and fell on the man hiding there.

Room for One More

by Kevin Crossley-Holland

How difficult it was to sleep in that strange bed! She wrestled with the duvet and thumped the pillow; she turned her back on the flimsy curtains; she wished she had never come up to London.

At midnight she heard the grandfather clock whirr and strike; and then she heard the gravel in the driveway crunch. At once she jumped out of bed and crossed the room and just peeped between the curtains.

What she could see was a gleaming black hearse. But there was no coffin in it, and no flowers. No, the hearse was packed out with living people: a crush of talking, laughing, living people.

Then the driver of the hearse looked straight up at her, as she peeped between the curtains.

'There's room for one more.' That's what he said. She could hear his voice quite clearly. Then she tugged the curtains so they crossed over, and ran back across the room, and jumped into bed, and pulled the duvet up over her head. And when she woke up next morning, she really wasn't sure whether it was all a dream or not.

That day, she went shopping. In the big store, she did Levi's Jeanswear on the fifth floor; she did Adidas Sportswear and that was on the sixth floor; and then she did cosmetics and that was on the seventh floor. Carrying two bags in each hand, she walked over to the lift. But when the bell pinged and the doors opened, she saw the lift was already jammed full with people.

The lift attendant looked straight at her as she stood there with her bags. 'There's room for one more,' he said. And his face was the face of the driver of the hearse.

'No,' she said quickly. 'No, I'll walk down.'

Then the lift doors closed with a clang. At once there was a kind of grating screech, and a terrible rattling, then a huge double thud.

The lift in the big store dropped from top to bottom of the shaft, and every single person in it was killed.

Buddha and the Swan

retold by Robert Fisher

Buddha was born more than 2500 years ago in northern India. He was a prince, the son of a rich king, and his name was Siddhartha. When he was born, his father sent for wise men and priests to foretell the baby prince's future. One said that he would become a great emperor, another said he would become a holy man. The last said that he would leave home and become a great teacher when he found out about old age, sickness and death. The king wanted his son to be a great emperor, not a monk or teacher. So he gave orders that the prince should grow up never knowing about old age, illness or death.

When Siddhartha was a boy he was never allowed out of the royal palace, and he never saw people who were old, ill or unhappy. Even dying flowers were picked from the royal gardens so that he would not see them. All he knew about were his rich family, their servants in the palace, and the animals that lived in the palace grounds. The young prince learned how to read and write, how to ride a horse and how to shoot a bow and arrow. He became very good at these things, so much so that his cousin Devadatta became very jealous of him.

Even when he was young Siddhartha had a compassionate nature. Here is what happened when he found for the first time an animal that was suffering.

* * * * *

* * * * *

One day, when Siddhartha was with his cousin in the palace grounds, they saw a swan. Devadatta reached for his bow and arrow, took careful aim and shot the bird.

'Look at that!' said Devadatta. 'Shot him first time!'

The great white bird fell bleeding to the ground. As soon as he saw the swan fall, Siddhartha ran over to it and carefully pulled out the arrow. He took some leaves and began to wipe the blood away. He nursed the bird in his arms, stroking its white feathers.

'Take your hands off my swan!' shouted Devadatta. 'You've no right to touch it. It's my swan. I shot it!'

'Yes,' said Siddhartha. 'But I'm trying to save it.'

'That's not fair,' said Devadatta. 'It's mine. I shot it. You must give it to me. If you don't give it back I'll take you to court.'

'All right,' said the prince. 'We'll let the court decide.'

Devadatta and Siddhartha went before the judge in the royal courtyard of the palace. Whilst they were waiting, Siddhartha refused to be parted from the swan. He kept it with him, nursing it in his arms. Now it was up to the judge to decide. Who should the swan be given to? To Devadatta who had shot it, or to the prince who had tried to save it?

The judge looked carefully at the swan, and saw that it was recovering from its wound. He then gave his judgement. As the swan was alive, due to the care of the prince, he should be allowed to keep it. Otherwise it would have died, and then Devadatta who had shot it could have claimed it.

After some time, the swan recovered completely, and the prince set it free again. All his life, Siddhartha cared for animals. He would never kill living beings, and he told his followers that they should kill no living things. This was Buddha's first teaching.

WHO?

by Chris Buckton

The face at the window looked somehow familiar to Jake. It was a boy's face, about the same age as him. It was always at the window, half hidden behind the curtain, as Jake walked past the house. He'd never seen the boy playing out. The face had a mournful look; maybe the boy was ill, and stuck in his room all day.

Jake asked his mum. 'Who lives at number six?'

'Oh, that's the house which we nearly bought last year. It's bigger than ours – more of a garden too. We couldn't afford it, though – like living in an alternative universe, I reckon! Dreamland!'

But Jake was curious about the boy. 'Who lives there now?'

'It's empty.'

'But there's a boy …'

His mum hardly listened.

The next time he went past, he tried waving. The boy mirrored his action.

Jake smiled.

The boy smiled.

I guess he must be lonely, thought Jake. Maybe I should knock on the door. He looks so sad.

But something made him hesitate. It wasn't until the boy beckoned to him the following day that he decided he would knock. After all, if the boy turned out to be a drag, Jake could leave it there. They didn't have to be friends for ever or anything. And he did feel curious …

It was the boy who opened the door. Was he on his own, then? Thoughts of runaways and hostages began to race through Jake's head.

'Hi. I'm Jake. I saw you at the window …' Jake's

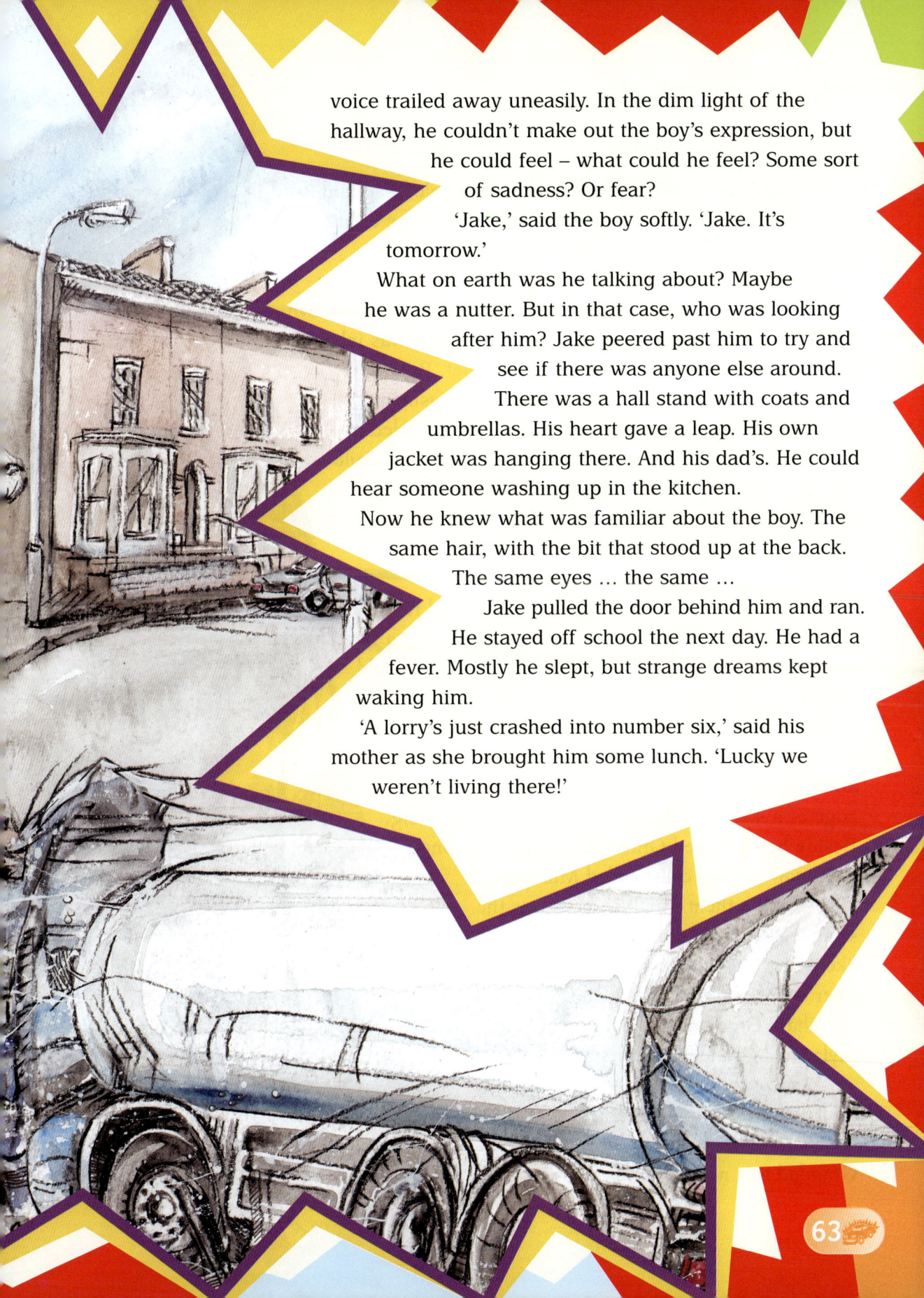

voice trailed away uneasily. In the dim light of the hallway, he couldn't make out the boy's expression, but he could feel – what could he feel? Some sort of sadness? Or fear?

'Jake,' said the boy softly. 'Jake. It's tomorrow.'

What on earth was he talking about? Maybe he was a nutter. But in that case, who was looking after him? Jake peered past him to try and see if there was anyone else around.

There was a hall stand with coats and umbrellas. His heart gave a leap. His own jacket was hanging there. And his dad's. He could hear someone washing up in the kitchen.

Now he knew what was familiar about the boy. The same hair, with the bit that stood up at the back. The same eyes … the same …

Jake pulled the door behind him and ran.

He stayed off school the next day. He had a fever. Mostly he slept, but strange dreams kept waking him.

'A lorry's just crashed into number six,' said his mother as she brought him some lunch. 'Lucky we weren't living there!'

The Last Thylacine

by Jan Andrew Henderson

Grandad was small and brown like a crumpled bag and lived in a home. Dad made me visit once a month, though he didn't come much himself. He said they didn't get on.

When Dad was my age, Grandad took him and Gran to Australia to seek their fortune. He was going to have his own fish van, like at home, because a lot of Australia was inland and he thought they'd appreciate a balanced diet. But he overslept on the boat and they ended up in Tasmania.

There weren't many people there and fish tended to go off quickly in the heat, so he never got rich. He could only afford a tiny wooden shack near the beach. It got too much for Gran and eventually they all came back. My dad still hates the seaside and he can't pass a garden shed without wincing.

When I arrived at the home last week I had to tie my dog to the railings outside – he wouldn't hurt a fly, but he was quite big and I suppose that scared the old people.

Grandad was sitting in a tatty robe, looking at old photographs. Some were of Gran before she passed away. I picked one up. Gran was standing on the edge of a steamy Tasmanian forest, looking young. Beside her frolicked Grandad's own dog – long dead now – a big collie called Mumphy.

Watching them from the trees was the strangest-looking animal I'd ever seen. It looked like a dog too, but it had a huge gaping jaw and tiger stripes up its back.

'That,' Grandad said solemnly, 'is a thylacine.' Grandad rarely smiled.

'What's a thylacine?'

'Look it up on that internet thing.'

Then he went back to his pictures. Grandad was never one for talking.

a thylacine

So I did. According to the website, thylacines were also called Tasmanian wolves. And the last ever thylacine died in Hobart Zoo in 1936.

I knew that Grandad was old, but he wasn't that old. I ran back to the home.

'You found a living thylacine in Tasmania!' I said. 'You could have been rich after all. You could have been famous!'

'I didn't tell anyone,' he replied. 'The authorities would just have dragged the poor creature off to a zoo.' He picked up the photograph and sighed. I couldn't tell if he was looking at the last thylacine or at Gran.

'All he wanted was what I wanted,' Grandad said. 'A bit of freedom and perhaps a fine grandson.' Then he put the photograph back in his old shoebox and shut the lid.

I went outside. My own dog, Mumphy III, was still tied to the railings and barked happily when he saw me. He was a collie cross – his mother and his mother's mother had all belonged to my family.

Mumphy III had tufty fur and pricked-up ears like all collies – but there were darker bands on his back and legs – I always thought that they looked a bit weird. He gave a wide yawn and I noticed for the first time that his jaw was awfully large.

I glanced up at the windows of the home. Grandad was watching from behind the glass.

He smiled, just once, and gave a little bow.

Rights

Introduction

Rights are the things people are allowed to do or have. Rights can be different for different groups of people. They can be affected by things like your age, or where you live, or what job you do. Throughout history, people have been fighting for their rights.

Should you be able to vote at 16?

Voting is something that everybody does. We vote for lots of different things. Sometimes your family might not be able to decide where to go on holiday, so you could take a quick vote, with each person saying what they want. Some schools have a council, and all the pupils vote for children they want to be on it.

In Britain, once you become 18, you can also vote for the people you want to help run the country. They are called Members of Parliament (MPs). They belong to political parties. General elections are held so that people can decide which MP they want to represent them. The party with the most MPs that have been chosen forms a government. The leader of that party becomes prime minister.

Lots of grown-ups think that 16-year-olds should be able to vote in general elections. They point out that you can join the army at 16 and die for your country. You can also, if your parents agree, get married at 16 (and in Scotland, if you are 16, you can get married without asking your parents).

If you start work at 16 you have to pay taxes, which are used to help run the country. But you are not allowed to vote – to have a say in who runs the country and spends your taxes, – until you are 18.

BALLOT BOX

Voting is anonymous; nobody ever knows who you have voted for – unless you tell them!

In Britain before 1928, women didn't have the same voting rights as men. A group of women called suffragettes didn't think this was right, and fought until women were given the right to vote.

⊛ People aged 16 can vote in eight countries – including Brazil, Croatia and the Philippines – but not in any European Union country. Iran has a voting age of 15.

⟨⟨Hi, my name is John. I left school at 16 and joined the army nine months later. I got married to my girlfriend and I pay tax on my wages. That tax helps the government pay for all the things we need, like the health service and schools. But I'm not 18 yet, so I can't vote. I don't have any say in how this country is run. Is that right?⟩⟩

VOTING FACTS

⊛ The voting age was last lowered in 1970, from 21 to 18.

⊛ Women were given the same right to vote as men on 2nd July, 1928. They had campaigned for 61 years to get it.

Corps: infantry
Status: soldier
Gender: male
Minimum age:
16 years 9 months
Maximum age:
26 years 11 months
Minimum service:
4 years.
Your main job during wartime will be to fight with and defeat the enemy – you will be in the thick of the action.

"There is obviously a case for saying: 'Look, people grow up a lot more quickly ... so why shouldn't you be able to vote?'"
Tony Blair, Prime Minister, 3rd December 2003

Q: Should we be able to vote at the age of 16? Or should we wait until 18 before we can marry or join the army?

At 16, you can become a soldier and fight for your country – but you can't vote.

Why do we have to wear a uniform?

Many people wear uniforms. Uniforms can tell you who a person is. Soldiers, sailors and airmen wear uniforms. So do police officers, doctors, nurses and paramedics. Traders on some financial exchanges wear special colourful jackets so that people they are dealing with can easily see them and know what company they work for.

Uniforms are worn for different reasons.

Uniforms can be protective – think of a firefighter's helmet or a roadside recovery person's reflective coat.

Music and religious uniforms

Uniforms can also show what kind of music you like to listen to – think of rap stars, punks or hippies. Or even what religion you follow – think of vicars, Catholic priests or the Muslim burka.

Did you know ...?

⊛ Lawyers called barristers have to wear a wig and gown in court. If they don't, the judge pretends not to see them.

⊛ Men's ties were first worn by Chinese warriors in the 2nd century BC.

⊛ Policemen's helmets were introduced in the 19th century to replace their top hats.

School uniforms

School pupils wear uniforms:

⭐ to show which school they are at;

⭐ to encourage a feeling of team spirit and togetherness;

⭐ to look smart.

Until the 1960s and 70s, most school uniforms meant trousers for boys and skirts or gymslips for girls. Both had to wear ties and blazers.

School uniform in the 1960s

As time went on, these school uniforms began to look more and more out of date, and schools began to get fed up with the way pupils were altering their clothes to make them look more fashionable. Soon, more modern clothes like school sweatshirts and fleece jackets were introduced by many schools.

Q: Are uniforms important? Why can't we just wear what we want?

Lots of schools still expected girls to wear skirts, and it was not until 2000 that girls all over Britain were allowed to wear trousers to school. This happened when Jo Hale – then aged 14 – won a three-year battle with her school, in Gateshead, which had banned girls from wearing trousers.

School uniform in 2004

What's so good about going to school?

School in India

School in America

Not everybody in the world goes to school. Some countries are too poor to make sure there are enough schools for all their children.

In some countries, governments don't care if poor people don't get educated. If poor people can't read or write then they can be made to work hard for very little money. They can be exploited.

* Around 113 million children worldwide do not go to school; two-thirds of them are girls.
* Africa spends three times as much on repaying its debts to other countries as on education.
* India spends twice as much on arms as on education.

Some countries feel that it is more important for boys to go to school than for girls. In some places, girls are still expected to stay at home and look after their families.

Kofi Annan, leader of the United Nations, has said, 'When the choice has to be made between educating a boy and a girl, the girl is more likely to stay at home. When a family needs extra income, the girl is more likely to be sent to work.'

Governments 'shall ... make primary education compulsory and available to all.'
UN Convention on the Rights of the Child, 12th December 1989

In rich countries, like Britain, every child gets an education. But why do we go to school? Is it just so that we can get jobs when we leave? Why do we have to spend six hours a day, five days a week for twelve years at school? Surely it doesn't take that long to learn to read and write? (Can you work out how many hours you will have spent at school by the time you leave?)

'I learned from my friends how to sniff glue. I saw them sniffing and that gave me a feeling that I would like to do it too. But we are not to blame. Our families are to blame. Had we been brought up properly and educated, nothing like it would have happened to us. We would have felt that we were girls like other girls walking by. Whenever I see a girl going to school, I feel sorry for myself because I haven't been to school and haven't been educated like her.'
Heba, 15, Egypt

Staying at home

Every child from the age of five in Britain has to be educated. But some parents choose to educate their children at home instead of at school.

One parent says, 'It's not that I feel that school is a good idea gone wrong, but a wrong idea from the word go. It's a nutty notion that we can have a place where nothing but learning happens, cut off from the rest of life.'

But not everybody can be educated at home. What about:

⊛ parents who can't afford to stop working?
⊛ parents who might be useless at teaching?

Q: Why don't we have more time off to do sport or painting, or just to play?

71

We know our rights – so what?

From the moment we are born we have rights. There are laws to protect us, to punish people who harm us, to make sure our food and water are clean and safe, to ensure that we get an education.

When we are babies and small children we are not expected to do anything in return, but as we grow older we get responsibilities. And lots of us don't like them very much.

Are any of these your responsibilities:

⊛ tidying your bedroom?
⊛ washing the dishes?
⊛ remembering to clean the guinea pig's cage?

Helping out in the family is all part of learning to cooperate with other people, which we will have to do when we grow up and leave home.

Human beings have always found that it is easier to survive as members of a group. When families banded together, it was easier to hunt, to share skills in making things, and to look after children and old people. Tribes in some countries today still live like this.

In western countries like Britain, this kind of living has become a bit more complicated.

People who give

We also have responsibilities to each other. We have big responsibilities, like not killing people, and smaller ones like being honest. But sometimes it is hard to know what to do for the best.

Some people spend their whole lives working for others.

⊛ Mother Theresa of Calcutta spent her life looking after the poor and sick in the slums of India.

⊛ Albert Schweitzer gave up a wealthy life to train as a doctor and work in Africa.

⊛ Many school leavers work for free for a year helping people in Africa, Asia or South America before they go to university.

What do you think?

When we work, we pay part of our wages to the government. This is called tax and it is used to pay for people and things that we all need, like doctors and the police force and roads and refuse collectors.

But grown-ups are always arguing about what our taxes should be spent on.

⊛ Until 1945, everybody had to pay to see a doctor. Now we all get free health care. Is this a good or bad idea?

⊛ Everybody knows that smoking and drinking too much is bad for you. If someone gets sick because they harm themselves, should they pay for their treatment at hospital?

⊛ Everybody knows that eating too many sweets is bad for your teeth. If you have to have lots of fillings, should your parents pay the dentist's fees?

What do we have a right to?

Q: **What are our responsibilities?**

73

Is advertising bad for us?

Children see about 20,000 television advertisements each year, many more than their parents do.

Businesses spend millions of pounds on advertising aimed at children, but there are no laws about how these adverts should be done.

Many people feel that children, especially young ones, just accept what they are told. They often can't tell the difference between a cartoon programme on television and a cartoon advert. Young children are attracted by adverts showing cuddly characters, and older children find adverts with catchy music or celebrities hard to resist.

Q: Do you think advertising should be banned during children's TV?

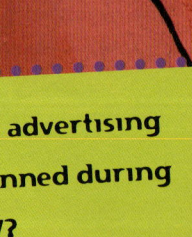

Many adverts are aimed at children.

We want it

Advertisers argue that:

⭐ parents can always switch off the TV and they don't have to give in to their children's pestering;

⭐ children's advertising is too complex to ban altogether. For example, is a toy advert in a comic acceptable but the same advert on television unacceptable?

⭐ children watch programmes – like football matches – that are often for adults too. How could you stop children seeing adverts meant for adults only?

No we don't

Politicians who want to ban advertising for toys and sweets during children's TV programmes say:

⭐ many of the food and drinks advertised are things that children should cut down on, like sugary cereals, sweets, fizzy drinks and burgers;

⭐ many of the toys shown aren't really that interesting, but are expensive;

⭐ children can be led to imagine that the toys they see on TV are better than they actually are;

⭐ children who see these adverts are being unfairly treated because they are easy to impress;

⭐ parents are pestered by their children into buying things they can't really afford.

What can we do about bullying?

Nearly everyone is bullied at some time in their lives: by brothers and sisters, by neighbours, by adults or by other children. But no one deserves to be bullied – and there are things you can do to stop it.

Some people who are now very successful adults were bullied in some way at school. They include Ms Dynamite, Tom Cruise, Gareth Gates, David Beckham and DJ Sarah Cox.

Bullying in school

Some schools used to turn a blind eye to bullying and, in years gone by, many children were just told by parents or teachers to stand up for themselves. Even today, many children don't feel that they are being taken seriously when they say they are being bullied.

> The children's charity Kidscape suggests the following:

> If you're being bullied, remember – it's not your fault.

How you can cope

⚛ Tell a friend what is happening. Ask him or her to help you. It will be harder for the bully to pick on you if you have a friend with you for support.

⚛ Try to ignore the bullying or say 'No' really firmly, then turn and walk away. Don't worry if people think you are running away. Remember, it is very hard for the bully to go on bullying someone who won't stand still to listen.

⚛ Try not to show that you are upset or angry. Bullies love to get a reaction – it's 'fun'. If you can keep calm and hide your emotions, they might get bored and leave you alone. As one teenager said to us, 'they can't bully you if you don't care'.

⚛ Don't fight back if you can help it. Most bullies are bigger or stronger than you. If you fight back you could make the situation worse, get hurt or be blamed for starting the trouble.

⚛ Try to avoid being alone in the places where you know the bully is likely to pick on you. This might mean changing your route to school, avoiding parts of the playground, or only using common rooms or lavatories when other people are there. It's not fair that you have to do this, but it might put the bully off.

⚛ Keep a diary of what is happening. Write down details of the incidents and your feelings. When you decide to tell someone, a written record of the bullying makes it easier to prove what has been going on.

> If you need any more information on bullying, you can contact organisations like Kidscape.

Rights by Helena Pielichaty

27, Shakespeare Street
Hodstock-on-Trent
LE12 8AS

To:
The Editor
Hodstock Gazette
Kirkgate
Hodstock-on-Trent
LE12 8AD

5th March

Dear Sir,

My name is Cesca Harrison and I am the Year Seven Representative on the Hodstock High School Student Council. I am writing to complain about the way you reported our demonstration last week ('School Goes on Strike', 27th February).

In my opinion, it was a very unfair piece. For starters, the headline was wrong. The Year Sevens weren't on *strike*; we hadn't refused to go to lessons or anything like that. All we were doing was protesting, in our own free time, about being banned from going into town at lunchtimes for a *whole term*, because of complaints from members of the public about the bad behaviour of four of our pupils. That's four out of two hundred!

We couldn't believe it when Mr Mason, our head of year, announced the ban in assembly. Why should we all be punished just because of a few nutters? I know for a fact that one of the nutters, Damien Craig, is in Year Eight, but they weren't banned, only the Year Sevens. That's ageist, but Mr Mason wouldn't listen; he never does. The protest was the only way of showing him how serious we were about losing our rights, especially as most of us only chose Hodstock High because it was so close to town in the first place.

Your report got a lot of other things wrong, too. We weren't 'chanting slogans' at all; we were singing songs from Bugsy Malone to make up for missing Mr Rudzig's rehearsal. Nor were we 'harassing passers-by'. We were just asking them to sign our petition to send to the European Court of Human Rights. OK, Rose Beattie did shout at one of the passers-by, but that doesn't count, because she was shouting at her sister, Michela, who had borrowed her jacket without asking.

The other thing you focused on was the 'atrocious' spelling on the placards. For your information, Billy Boy Bowman made them and he's dyslexic. It was mean of the report to make fun of him by saying: 'it is obvious some pupils can ill afford to spend time out of the classroom.' Billy Boy spends a lot of additional time in classrooms, actually, just catching up on stuff.

Anyway, what you should have been noticing was the words themselves, not the way they were spelled. Your reporter's as bad as my nan when the news is on. Instead of listening to what the newscaster is announcing, she says things like, 'Why is he wearing that terrible tie?' or, 'That shade of lemon does nothing for her complexion.' Talk about missing the point.

To summarise, therefore, please ask your reporter to interview all the people involved next time, not just the teachers – and lay off dyslexic people.

Yours faithfully,
Cesca Harrison 7ML

PS My full name is Francesca but I prefer Cesca, just in case you need to know, or think I am hiding behind an alias.

PPS On second thoughts, it's probably best not to print my name at all. Put something like 'full name and address supplied' like you do sometimes. It's not that I'm ashamed of what I've written, it's just that Mr Mason is my geography teacher and I don't want my grades to suffer. Thanks.

Get your facts right.

we ar hyumns not ammuls

79

Celebrate your Senses

Coming to our senses

We have five senses. We can see, hear, smell, taste and touch. Our senses help us live - they take in information about the world around us and tell our brains what is going on.

Think how impossible it would be to live if we had no senses at all. We use them so much that, often, we take them for granted. But imagine what it would be like if you suddenly went deaf or blind; if you could never hear your favourite music, or see people's faces any more. What about if you lost another sense - your taste, or smell, or touch? How could you enjoy a pizza, your favourite perfume - or even walk properly? After all, when you're walking you need to feel the ground under your feet.

We use our senses so much that we talk about them all the time. How many sayings can you think of involving your senses?

Out of sight, out of mind

I smell a rat

NOSY PARKER

Sight

Our eyesight is often thought of as the most important sense. It is an amazing thing - we can tell the difference between millions of shades of colour and recognise our friends from the slightest glance.

Seeing is believing.

Hearing

Hearing is thought of as the next most important sense. Our ears can handle anything from the heart-stopping roar of a low-flying jet to the rustle of a leaf. Our ears and our eyes get us out of danger all the time. Think how difficult it would be to even cross a road without them.

Touch

But our other senses are important too. We rely on our sense of touch to tell us when something is too hot or too cold. If we felt no pain, we might not realise that we were touching something that was dangerous. The nerve endings in our skin also allow us to tell how firmly we should hold something. Once nerve endings send information to our brains, our brains can quickly work out how to handle a snowflake or a hammer.

Taste and Smell

Our senses of taste and smell are closely related. Our tongues can only tell the difference between four basic tastes, but our noses know the difference between 10,000 smells.

Scientists think they may have discovered a sixth sense. They have found that people often have a feeling about something that they can't quite explain. It's like when you go into a room and have a feeling something has changed, but you're not sure what, or when you have a feeling something is about to happen before it does. Some people are calling this sixth sense 'mindsight'.

The eyes have it

Our eyes are complicated and delicate. When we look at an object, light bounces off it into our eyes. Our eyes gather and focus this light and change it into millions of nerve signals. These signals are sent down the optic nerve to the brain, which makes sense of it, and forms it into an image.

Your retina (the part of the eye that changes light into nerve signals) has 137 million light-sensitive cells all crammed into an area smaller than a postage stamp.

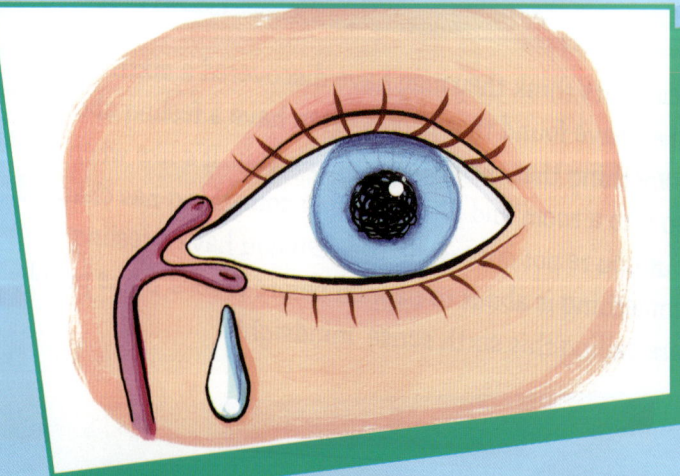

The busiest muscles in our bodies are the six in each of our eyes. These muscles make our eyes move about 100,000 times each day. That's as much exercise as leg muscles get on an 80-km walk.

Trick of the eye

But our brains can be fooled. When our eyes see unusual images, our brains may not be able to make sense of them in the usual way. The results can be very confusing!

How many legs does this elephant have?

What do you see when you look at this picture – a rabbit or a duck? (Here's a helpful hint: the rabbit faces one way, and the duck the other.)

Eye don't believe it!

◎ Tears clean your eyes; they are salty and contain something called lysozome, which kills germs. When you cry, tears drain into those tiny little holes in the corner of your eyes, and eventually end up in your nose – which is why your nose gets all runny when you cry.

◎ The average person blinks about 12 times a minute. That's 10,080 blinks in a 14-hour day. Every time you blink, your eyelid spreads an oily cleanser over the surface of your eye which stops it drying out.

◎ People who are colour-blind can't see things in as many colours as other people, and they cannot see certain colours like red, green and some blues.

◎ An eagle can see a rabbit about 2km away. A person could probably only spot a rabbit from a third of that distance.

◎ If you are short-sighted you can see things that are close very well, but you might have difficulty looking at things in the distance. The proper word for short-sightedness is myopia. People who are long-sighted can see things clearly far away, but can't see things close-up. This is called hyperopia.

Let's hear it for our ears

Hearing is thought to be the next most important sense after sight. Your ears work because of the way your eardrums vibrate when sound reaches them. Eardrums are membranes stretched between your outer ear – the little canal you can put your finger in – and your inner ear.

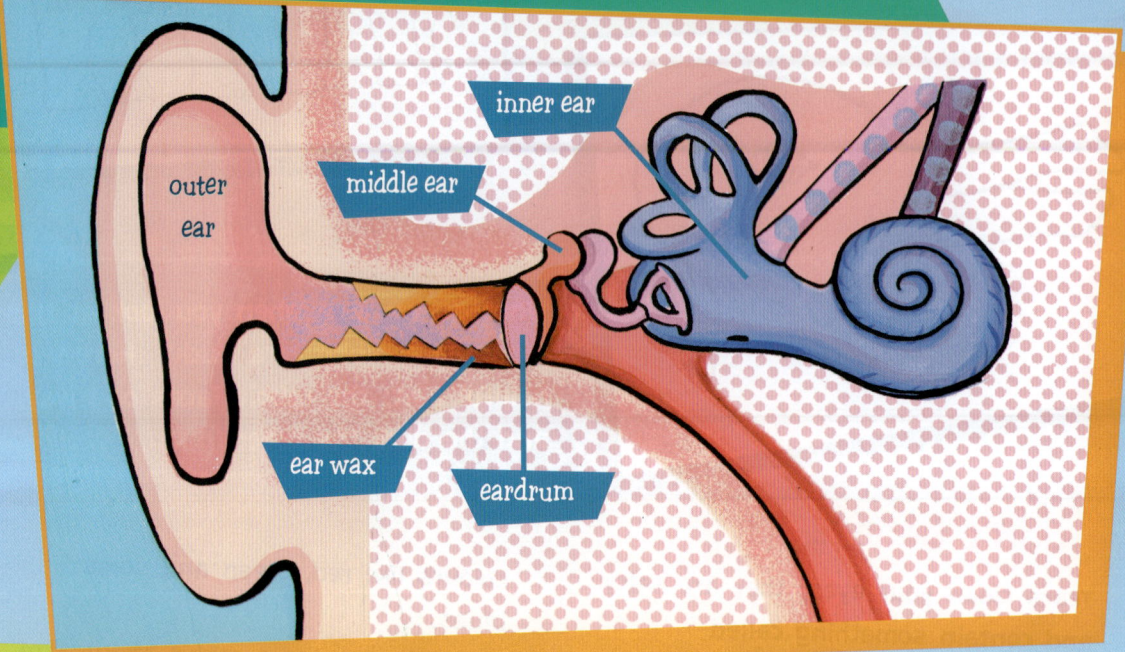

outer ear

middle ear

inner ear

ear wax

eardrum

Our hearing suffers when sound waves can't reach the inner ear. Too much earwax can stop sound waves.

Sneaky sound effects

Without sight, you can fool your ears. Sound-effects people have been doing this for years on the radio and in films. (They're called sound men in radio, and foley artists in film.)

These are some of the sounds they make - and how they make them:

◎ crackling fire - twisting cellophane;
◎ boiling water - blowing through a straw into water;
◎ skating on ice - rubbing two table knives together;
◎ breaking eggs - squeezing folded sandpaper;
◎ breaking glass - dropping a handful of tiny pieces of sheet metal onto board.

When the eardrum moves, so do little bones inside your ear. These bones make sounds louder and send the sound waves into a part of the inner ear where special cells change the sound into nerve signals. These signals are passed down your hearing nerve to your brain, which makes sense of what it hears.

Your voice sounds different when you hear it on a tape recorder because the sound reaches you only through the air. When you talk, some of the sound travels through the bones of your skull.

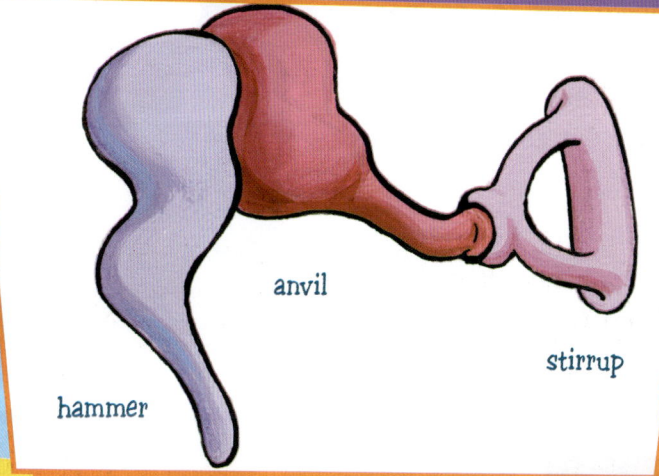

anvil

stirrup

hammer

The bones of the middle ear

Owl sounds

Scientists in America have discovered that snowy owls depend completely on their ears, and not their eyes, when hunting in the dark. The owls can tell where a mouse is because, when they hear it, they get slightly different information in each ear, which means that they can keep altering their position until it sounds the same in both ears – which means they are right on top of the mouse.

Rising to the challenge

If we lose one of our senses, often our other senses will try to make up for it. If we go blind, for example, our hearing often becomes sharper.

Ludwig van Beethoven

Ludwig van Beethoven is one of the greatest composers the world has ever known, yet for at least half his life, he was completely deaf. He was forced to rely on his imagination, and it is said he even had the legs taken off his piano so that he could feel the vibrations it made on the floorboards.

In 1824, at the premiere of his Ninth Symphony, he stood facing the orchestra, conducting, but at the end, when people shouted and clapped increasingly loudly to show their appreciation, he had to be turned round so that he could see their reaction.

Evelyn Glennie

Sound is simply vibrating air which the ear picks up and changes to signals that our brains make sense of. As well as hearing vibrations, we can also feel them. This means that even someone who is deaf (like Beethoven) can still 'hear' sounds through touch.

Evelyn Glennie uses touch to feel the vibrations of musical instruments so that she can play music. She feels low sounds in her legs and feet, and high sounds on her face, neck and chest.

Percussionist Evelyn Glennie 'hears' music through touch.

Louis Braille

Louis Braille showed how the sense of touch can make up for lack of sight. Louis was blinded in an accident in his father's workshop when he was three years old. He was so clever that he still managed to stay top of the class at his village school in Coupvray, near Paris.

At the age of 10, he won a scholarship to a special college for the blind in Paris. The college had just 14 books made with special raised letters for the blind to read. But it took even the brightest person several minutes just to read a sentence.

Then, Louis heard about a new system of raised letters that soldiers used when they wanted to send messages at night without being seen. He adapted it, but it was not until after he died, in 1852, that his Braille system became used all over the world. With it, a blind person can read just as quickly as a sighted one.

Here is the Braille system of letters. If you copy them, and then put dots of glue on the spots, you will have made your own Braille alphabet. See if you can make and read some messages.

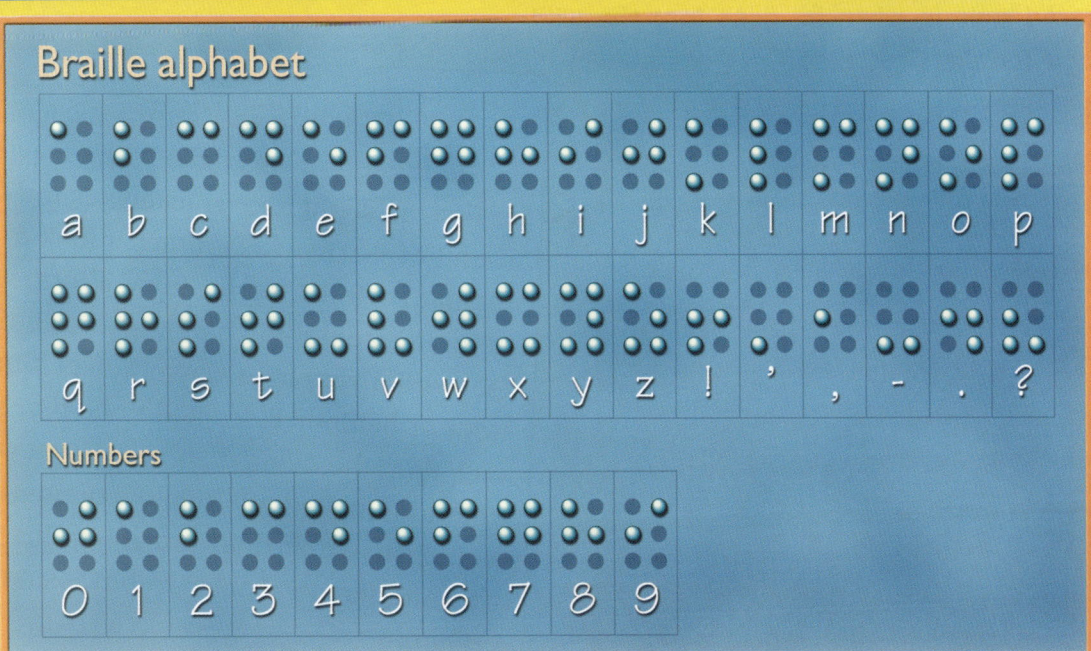

Braille alphabet

a b c d e f g h i j k l m n o p

q r s t u v w x y z ! ' , - . ?

Numbers

0 1 2 3 4 5 6 7 8 9

A feeling for art

Our senses help us to make sense of the world around us, but we can also use them to show others how we feel. Writers, artists and musicians do this all the time. The best artists don't paint pictures that look like photographs; their paintings actually give us a sense of being in the picture, of feeling the heat, the light, the emotion.

Writers try to get us to feel the same way their characters do, by appealing to our senses. If, for example, you want to write about somebody being scared in a forest at night, you could just say, 'He heard noises and he was scared.' It's accurate, but does it make you feel as though you are that frightened person?

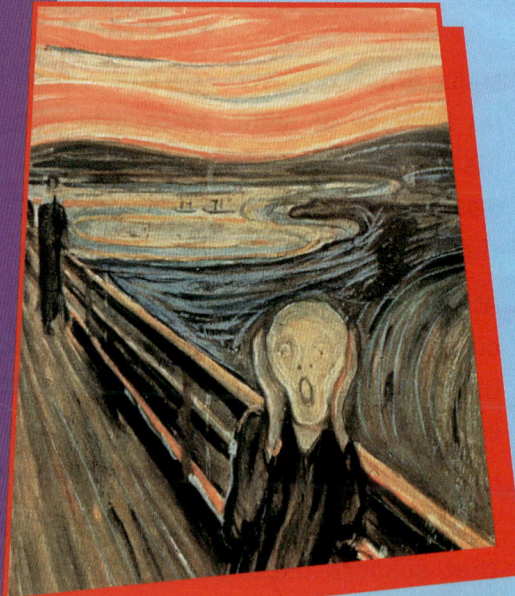

Edvard Munch wants us to feel the emotion in his painting *The Scream*.

Look at this passage by Kenneth Grahame, from *The Wind in the Willows*, and see how he uses the sense of hearing to show how scared Mole is when he goes into the Wild Wood for the first time.

The artist Monet wants us to feel the light and heat in this garden.

Then the pattering began.

He thought it was only falling leaves at first, so slight and delicate was the sound of it. Then, as it grew, it took a regular rhythm, and he knew it for nothing else but the pat-pat-pat of little feet, still a very long way off. Was it in front or behind? It seemed to be first one, then the other, then both. It grew and it multiplied, till from every quarter as he listened anxiously, leaning this way and that, it seemed to be closing in on him.

Sense poems

Sense poems are five-verse poems that describe abstract emotions and ideas – like fear – using each of the five senses. Here's an example:

When I think of wishes,
I see glittering meteors crossing the silent blue sky.

When I think of wishes,
I hear the grand concerto performed by the ocean at dawn near the shore.

When I think of wishes,
I taste the most delicious cake in the world that someone dear baked specially for me.

When I think of wishes,
I smell the fragrant sakura when its petals fly past.

When I think of wishes,
I feel the gentle hands of my mother soothing me whenever I cried when I was a baby.

Jess Yim Ka-mei

Some poets describe the senses to make their poems seem more real.

Which senses are described in this poem?

Giant Winter

Giant Winter preys on the earth,
Gripping with talons of ice,
Squeezing, seeking a submission,
Tightening his grip like a vice.

Starved of sunlight shivering trees
Are bent by his torturing breath.
The seeds burrow into the soil
Preparing to fight to the death.

Giant Winter sneers at their struggles,
Blows blizzards from his frozen jaws,
Ripples cold muscles of iron,
Clenches tighter his icicle claws.

Just as he seems to be winning,
Strength suddenly ebbs from his veins.
He releases his hold and collapses.
Giant Spring gently takes up the reins.

Snarling, bitter with resentment,
Winter crawls to his polar den,
Where he watches and waits till it's time
To renew the battle again.

John Foster

Strange smells of success

The lives of dogs, and other animals, are ruled by smells. Some animals rely on smells to find food, to recognise trails and territory, and to identify their mate or offspring. Insects like ants send and receive smells that tell them exactly where to go and how to behave.

Human mothers can recognise their babies by smell, and newborn babies recognise their mothers in the same way.

The average human being can recognise up to 10,000 separate smells. But there is no recognised way of scientifically describing them. Scientists measure sound on wavelengths, but there is no 'smell length'. Think of some very strong smells, like petrol, aftershave, bread baking. How would you describe them?

The world's smelliest plant is the stinking corpse lily, which smells like rotten meat. It uses the pong to attract flies, which it eats.

Ants use their sense of smell to communicate with each other.

Smelling and tasting

We think that we can tell how a thing tastes by putting it on our tongue, but most of the flavour of food comes from its smell, which wafts up the nostrils and the back of the mouth to cells in the nose. That's why, if we have a cold, most food can seem pretty tasteless. All the same, it is the tongue, covered with bundles of nerve endings called taste buds, that sends the brain messages about what we are eating.

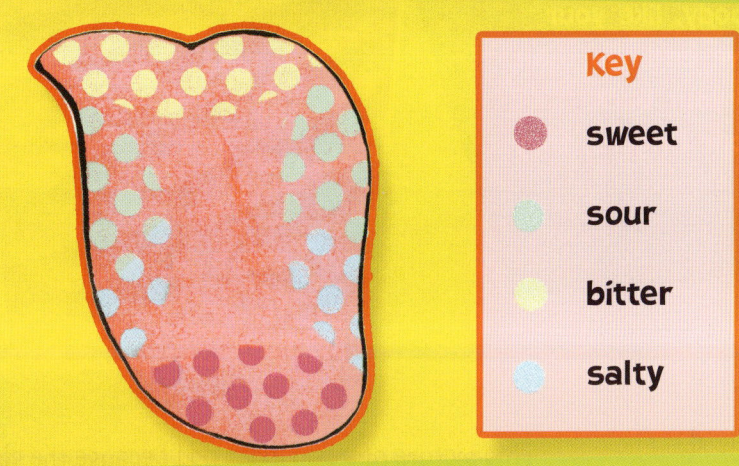

Key

● sweet

● sour

● bitter

● salty

Different tastes are tasted on different parts of your tongue.

Some scientists believe that, as well as the four basic tastes, the human tongue can detect a fifth taste. Called *umami* (a Japanese word), the description of the taste is hard to translate into English, but it has been described as 'savoury', 'essence', 'pungent', 'deliciousness' and 'meaty'!

This means that one very safe way of trying to find out if something is safe to eat, is by smelling it first. Our eyes often fool us. Some things can look beautiful - but can be very dangerous. If you don't know what something is, it's always best to check with a grown-up first.

This is one of the large bumps found on your tongue. Inside these bumps are taste buds.

In touch with our skin

The sense of touch comes from our skin. The epidermis, or the top layer of skin, contains many nerve endings all over your body. These nerve endings send messages to your brain telling you what kind of thing you are feeling (e.g. hot, cold, sharp, soft).

Particular parts of your body, like your fingertips, have more nerve endings than, for example, the small of your back. That's why, if you hurt your fingers, they *really* hurt.

This picture of a boy looks odd because the size of his body parts are drawn according to how many nerve endings they have.

When someone or something touches you, you can feel that it is touching you, but you can also feel that you touch it back. You can feel how hard something is touching you, too. We use special nerve endings to feel pressure. Sometimes, if we press too hard, we get a bruise on our skin.

Our sense of touch also allows us to feel pain. This is useful because it can stop us from hurting ourselves too badly - if we touch something that is hot, we immediately take our hand away.

Super skin

Skin is the largest organ in the body. It makes up nearly a fifth of an adult's weight, and it covers an area of about 18,000 cm². Every square centimetre has:

- 2.9 million cells;
- 3,000 sensory cells;
- 97 sweat glands;
- 14 oil glands;
- nearly 1 m of blood vessels;
- ... and lots of little bugs crawling all over it, eating the dead skin.

There will be over a million skin mites on you and around you right now, just like this one, chomping on your dead skin.

The skin that you see on the outside is all dead. You shed about 40,000 dead skin cells every minute – that's enough to fill a small suitcase in a lifetime. Most of the dust you breathe in is dead skin. Every time you blow your nose, there's a little bit of your friends and family (and you) in your hanky!

Skin facts

- Skin grows faster than any other organ. We keep making new skin for our whole lives.
- Skin is tough, elastic and waterproof. It is designed to keep our other organs in and germs out.
- Skin has two layers: the epidermis on top and the dermis below.
- You can help protect your skin by wearing a hat, suncream and sunglasses and by covering up your arms and legs.
- Hair and fingernails are also part of the skin, but they don't have nerve endings. This is why it doesn't hurt at all to cut them.

Some scientists think that touch is far more important than sight. Without it, how do you know where your body ends and something else begins?

Index

Unit 1
Extremity Man

Andes 15
Arctic 7, 10
Atacama Desert 15
Challenger Deep 6, 7
Cherrapunji 14
Chile 15
Death Valley 12–13
desert 12, 15
Everest, Mount 6, 16
fish, deep-sea 7, 8–9
gold mining 12
Hillary, Sir Edmund 16
India 14
Mariana Trench 6–9
Pacific Ocean 7, 15
Philippines 7
photophores 8
Piccard, Jacques 7
rain 12, 14, 15
Russia 10–11
Tenzing Norgay 16
Trieste 7
USA 12–13
Verkhoyansk 10–11
Walsh, Don 7

Unit 2
Something Wicked This Way Comes

Anglo-Dutch wars 27, 28
Charles II 32, 33
Defoe, Daniel 30
diaries 26–27, 28, 33
Dutch fleet 26, 27
Evelyn, John 28, 33
Great Fire of London 26, 29, 32–33
Great Plague 26, 27, 29–31, 32
London 19, 26, 27, 29, 32–33
Macbeth 20–25
obituaries 28
Pepys, Samuel 26–27, 28, 32
rats 29, 32
Shakespeare 18–19, 24–25, 26
Stratford-upon-Avon 18, 19

Unit 3
Carbon Copy

carbon 34, 35, 38, 39, 42, 44
carbon dioxide 35, 42
charcoal 34, 35, 36–37
coal 35, 38, 39, 42, 43
coal mining 39
diamonds 35, 44–45
dinosaurs 38
drawing 35, 36
Evelyn, John 37
firefighting 41
fossil fuels (hydrocarbons) 35, 38–39, 42
gas, natural 35, 38, 39, 40
global warming 42–43
graphite 34, 35, 36, 44
gunpowder 37
human beings 34, 42
Industrial Revolution 39, 42
North Sea 40, 41
oil 34, 35, 38, 39, 40–41, 42
oil wells 40, 41
petrol 34, 41, 42
pollution 37, 41, 42
power stations 42, 43
stars 34, 45
trees 35, 37, 42

Unit 4
Sensational shorts

No index needed (all fiction)

Unit 5
Rights

advertising 74–75
Africa 70, 72
army 66, 67
bullying 76–77
education 70–71, 72
governments 66, 67, 70,
    71, 73
health care 67, 73
India 70, 72
laws 72, 74
police 68, 73
politicians 66, 75
religion 68
responsibilities 72
school 66, 67, 69, 70–71,
    77, 78–79
Schweitzer, Albert 72
soldiers 67, 68
taxes 66, 67, 73
Teresa, Mother 72
uniforms 68–69
voting 66–67
work 66, 71, 72, 73

Unit 6
Celebrate Your Senses

art 88
Beethoven, Ludwig van 86
bones 85
Braille, Louis 87
brain 80, 81, 82, 83, 85, 86,
    91, 92
cells 85, 91, 93
colour 80, 83
eardrum 84, 85
ears 81, 84–85, 86
eyes 80, 81, 82–83, 85, 91
Glennie, Evelyn 86
hearing 80, 81, 84–85, 86,
    88
muscles 82
music 80, 86
nerves 81, 82, 85, 91, 92,
    93
nose 81, 83, 91, 93
pain 81, 92
sight 80, 82–83, 84, 87, 93
sixth sense 81
skin 81, 92–93
smell 80, 81, 90–91
sound 84, 85, 86, 90
taste 80, 81, 91
tongue 81, 91
touch 80, 81, 86, 87, 92–93